LEADERSHIP

---◆---

Impact, Culture, and Sustainability

Nancy S. Huber and
Michael Harvey, Editors

a volume in the International Leadership Association series
Building Leadership Bridges

THE INTERNATIONAL LEADERSHIP ASSOCIATION (ILA) is a global network for all those who practice, study, and teach leadership. The ILA promotes a deeper understanding of leadership knowledge and practices for the greater good of individuals and communities worldwide. The principal means by which this mission is accomplished is through the synergy that occurs by bringing together public- and private-sector leaders, scholars, educators, consultants, and students from many disciplines and many nations. For more information, please visit www.ila-net.org.

The ILA was founded by and is based at The James MacGregor Burns Academy of Leadership at the University of Maryland. The Burns Academy of Leadership fosters leadership through scholarship, education, and training, with special attention to advancing the leadership of groups historically underrepresented in public life. For more information, please visit www.academy.umd.edu.

The ILA partnered with the Center for Creative Leadership (CCL®) to produce this publication. CCL is a top-ranked, global provider of executive education that develops better leaders through its exclusive focus on leadership education and research. Founded in 1970 as a nonprofit, educational institution, CCL helps clients worldwide cultivate creative leadership—the capacity to achieve more than imagined by thinking and acting beyond boundaries—through an array of programs, products, and other services. CCL is headquartered in North America with campuses in Brussels and Singapore. For more information, visit www.ccl.org.

For additional copies of this book, please contact the publisher:

THE JAMES MACGREGOR BURNS ACADEMY OF LEADERSHIP
University of Maryland
College Park, MD 20742-7715 USA
Phone: 301-405-5218
Fax: 301-405-6402
E-mail: ila@ila-net.org
Web: www.ila-net.org

Library of Congress ISBN: 978-1-891464-28-7

Production: Center for Creative Leadership
Production Editor: Joanne Ferguson

Table of Contents

Introduction

The International Leadership Association is pleased to offer *Leadership: Impact, Culture, and Sustainability*, the newest volume in the Building Leadership Bridges series. The authors herein represent a diverse range of scholars, practitioners, and educators who offer some of the best contemporary thinking in the leadership arena.

In keeping with the mission of ILA, *Leadership: Impact, Culture, and Sustainability* seeks to integrate different experiences, traditions, and ways of thinking about leadership in the modern world. It is both a privilege and a challenge to peruse the submitted articles and choose from among a number of worthy entries those to be included in this year's volume. To enhance your reading, we begin with a "weaver's commentary" this year by invited author Barbara Mossberg. Her piece is a clever integration of various concepts found in this volume around the broader theme of building bridges. Inside you will discover topics that range from ethics to intuition, competition to communication, and a master's program to social enterprise and community development. We hope you enjoy the International Leadership Association's annual volume of written work contributed by members of our multifaceted organization!

The Building Leadership Bridges series is but one of several avenues to learn about the impact of leadership, its culture, and the sustainable practice of leadership. Please bookmark the ILA website—http://www.ila-net.org—and visit frequently for news and resources as well as dates and information about leadership events.

This volume would not be possible without the contributions of the authors. In addition, we would like to express our appreciation to others who partner with us in this effort. We are grateful to the Center for Creative Leadership for the expertise they provide in the production of a quality publication. Special thanks go to CCL's Joanne Ferguson whose diligence makes us all look good! Thanks are also offered to the ILA Board of Directors for their continuing support and encouragement of our attempts to evolve in ways we hope will better serve all of you who study, practice, teach, and care about leadership in the world.

Nancy S. Huber and Michael Harvey

Editors

The Bridge as a Powerful Metaphor— Where Is It Taking Us?
A Weaver's Commentary

By Barbara Mossberg

THIS COLLECTION IN A CONTINUING SERIES BRINGS TOGETHER— "bridges"—an assemblage of research documentation and analysis with the object of applying and extending current knowledge. Taken together, the articles identify common mandates, challenges, and opportunities for the leadership development field. Following is an individual response to and reflection on the deep structure of this collection as a whole, emergent from the various "pieces" by our authors—a meditation on the importance of the series' thematic purpose of building bridges.

Considering a series whose philosophy and metaphor is of bridging, we can step back in this volume to reflect on what we mean by bridges and the importance of this context for assessing our goals and achievements in leadership practice, development, and studies as evidenced in recent research studies. In fact, the concept of "bridges" illuminates a way leadership is an integral art and science, in which psychology, dynamical systems theories, sociology, and cognitive science productively fuse.

As a design solution to a perceived need and sense of possibility—promoting access and relations, getting from here to there, combining resources— a bridge is one of the most positive symbols of our creative powers. It is a work of utmost imagination, motivated by the desire to extend our reach, render irrelevant the sense of opposing "sides," overcome inherent obstacles. Embedded in the triumph of such a symbol is a core reality. A bridge is a practical way to connect things naturally separated, like people on opposite sides of a river.

"Something there is that doesn't love a wall" – Robert Frost
The bridge speaks to the same wistful impatience with whatever keeps people and human systems apart that Robert Frost describes in his poem "Mending Wall." On the

theory that too easy commerce between "fields" could cause conflict, he describes how people deliberately construct barriers to keep out, and in, different ideas about the world ("good fences make good neighbors"). Instead, a bridge is a counter-technology to facilitate such commerce and leverage difference for a greater common purpose. There is faith in such engineering in the human good that can result from a bridge.

Bridges, literally, were one of the first things occupying the human mind. Getting over naturally occurring breaks in the earth's surface—faster, easier, more efficiently—whether rocks in fissures and chasms, pieces of timber over creeks, or vine ropes over gulleys, led to efforts to replicate these naturally occurring bridges. Across the globe are ingenious and beautiful stone and timber structures, and later still, marvelous steel and concrete edifices that sway with air and earth currents. It is not too extreme to say that human history (and even ecological history) is a function of bridge making.

But engineering replicates natural bridges of another kind as well. Thinking is neural bridgework. Language is a technology that bridges minds. Art bridges vision. Metaphor connects things we don't think are remotely related. Metaphor allows us to conceive issues and problems as structurally similar if not also identical, and thus cleverly and resourcefully to adapt ways to resolve them; metaphor is the mind's efficiency tool, its transformer, its catalytic converter, its enzyme. The brain helplessly connects things as a survival principle — *that lobster is my food*. Equations are bridges to see how things belong together. Is not the genius in $e=mc^2$ the equals sign?

To consider a bridge is to celebrate the scope and agility of the human brain, which sees obstacles as "maybe not" and in Emily Dickinson's words is—speaking of metaphors—"wider than the sky."

Bridges as a Potent Image for Leadership Studies

The concept of bridges is developed in this volume in ways that particularly define scholarship's contributions to achievements and identifying challenges in today's organizations. As described by the various authors—in groups and individually representing different institutions, countries, and cultures—leaders not only promote, maintain, create, foster, build, and use bridges: leaders *are* bridges. This theory directly supports the premises of leadership scholarship and its purposes. Logically, the same ingenious and optimistic and even desperate thinking that goes into bridge design and development must go into leadership education and support. We have a great stake in building leaders who connect, withstand, and sustain great pressures to hold things together, are flexible and strong and enduring.

Further, bridges are presented as ways of thinking that allow us access to different kinds of knowledge that exist in different spheres; that enable communication and understanding among minds; that foster productive relationships and collabora-tions among groups. Any enterprise—whether a small business, a multinational, a school, a family, a country, a program, a summer camp, a theater production, a committee, a love relationship—is composed of entities that require a leader to build and support bridges among all the internal contributing units, and bridges to the external communities of which the organization is an integral part.

The Leader's Whole

In order to foster cooperation within the organization and to act in functional harmony in the larger social context, leaders must first envision and then engage with their community as a "whole." If we imagine looking at earth from space, we can see how things are connected that seem separated on the ground. It is only through seeing "the whole" that it is possible to see both what is intrinsically connected and what bridges need to be made and supported.

. . . Like Looking at Earth from Space

Within the leader's purview are elements that appear different in form and function. From space we see a continuous and coherent set of agricultural fields, wilderness forests, rivers, towns, deserts, high rises, lakes and seas, snow-capped peaks, freeways, marshes, pavement. It is night and day. We see different climates all occurring at once. We see people on horseback making their way on trails, we see people on elephants next to trucks and jeeps and Mercedes, we see computer terminals, we see temples, we see nurseries, and we see hospitals.

. . . A Complex Coherence

A "whole" is a system characterized by diversity, change, and complexity. Its parts function at different speeds and in different ways. In an organization, people may feel that the mission of their department has nothing to do with the mission of another: the mail room of a corporate headquarters has different operational day-to-day goals and challenges and costume and vocabulary than the health clinic; the maintenance and grounds crew are working with a different set of mandates and criteria for success than the technology support staff or the marketing executives or the legal counsel or the front office staff. The language and mental frameworks of the budget officers are a world apart, and require training in different educational sectors and disciplines, than the folks in the graphic arts department (or even the CEO office—ask any president about her CFO—or vice versa). Within departments factions exist, coalitions splinter and realign, and in the same field and methodology and theory-based entities, differences exist so extreme as to be comic or tragic.

...The Reality of Interdependence

How and why do these individuals and groups belong together? Leadership of the enterprise requires a view based on an understanding of the vital connections and similarities and interdependence of the groups and the systems within systems. It is not just "parallel play," as sociologists describe children on the playground engaged in different activities side by side and in the same timeframe. It is not just a neutral co-existence. Within one system, cultures can be seen to compete with and can be in opposition to each other. The conflict and tension that the narrator's neighbor in Robert Frost's poem "Mending Wall" feels is inevitable as intrinsic to human nature, can actually be a result of intentional policies, as when a university structures budget policy forcing departments to compete for funds and function at the expense of other departments and programs. No one can feel on the same side in such a structure, as English, math, law, the liberal arts, academics, special support services, and housing each fight for a slice of the pie (everyone ignores continuing education in the bungalow on the edge of campus).

While by definition the individual units in a system each have different problems and goals and training, the system as a whole is dependent on their functioning in an integrated and coherent way. For the whole enterprise to succeed, everyone needs to know not only their distinct roles, but also their own value to the organization, which fosters pride in one's work and behavior, ethics, responsibility, and resiliency. Knowing one's value to an organization depends upon understanding one's relation to the others that make up the organization as a whole.

Leadership Holds the Magic Mirror to
Individual Value and Community Integrity

The leader sees the bridges that make the organizational landscape a coherent enterprise with a common purpose. Generating this vision of interdependence and leveraged relationships defines the art—and heart—of leadership. The communication and expression of this vision fosters an ethos of shared purpose, values, mission, challenges, and criteria for success. This in turn develops the capacity of the organization to create and utilize the "bridges" that give it integrity.

The organization comprised of elements with necessarily different and often competing points of view, with units often lacking knowledge and understanding about the others—whether a globe or factory or school—depends upon a vision of a leader that can see individual roles as vitally connected in a way that makes everyone feel he or she belongs to a larger more complex "whole." Everyone needs to know his or her intrinsic value to an enterprise. The leader holds a magic mirror to the community, providing a context built from care and encouragement and belief in the whole purpose of the enterprise. In such a mirror, we people in the "group shot" of a leader's vision of our community experience ourselves as "beautiful," that is, of essential value.

Thus morale and capacity of any individual or unit in an organization are inextricably tied to how one understands oneself as related to other people, departments, and activities. But this perspective of a greater harmony of interrelationships is difficult to achieve up close when one is immersed within a unit that feels separate (for better or worse). It is a vision that requires distance, the kind of perspective that allows one to see how we are connected to elements—people, offices, ideas—that may not even be known or visible or seem relevant to us. A leader's bridge-making promotes an entire network of role extensions that increase an organization's capacity to function. In this way, we see a leader's role as illuminating bridges, integral pathways of knowledge of how each element has value to the whole, bridges that drive inter-functioning relations and build a sense of community.

Drawing upon the bridge metaphor, we can see that an understanding of one's value to an organization is a function of relational knowledge, resulting in respect and support for other entities contributing to "the whole." Building this conceptual bridge between what an individual has to contribute and the larger purpose of the enterprise as a whole is the leader's gift to both individuals and the community. To recognize this role gives us the opportunity to develop ways to enable these capacities in our leaders. Our research, scholarship, teaching, and training can support the imaginative, generative, and often healing and renewing vision of leaders working as bridge-makers on behalf of "the whole."

**❝ TO THE EXTENT THAT WE CAN DEFINE LEADERSHIP ❞
AS A BRIDGE THAT CONNECTS VITAL ELEMENTS OF
A SUSTAINABLE AND THRIVING SYSTEM OR
SOCIETY, WE HAVE A USEFUL WAY OF APPROACH-
ING THE FIELD OF LEADERSHIP STUDIES AND
DEVELOPMENT THAT DRAWS UPON RESEARCH
STUDIES FEATURED IN THIS VOLUME.**

A Values-Based Approach to Leadership Concepts

To the extent that we can define leadership as a bridge that connects vital elements of a sustainable and thriving system or society, we have a useful way of approaching the field of leadership studies and development that draws upon research studies featured in this volume. To examine further how the bridge metaphor serves understanding of mandates, opportunities, and challenges in the field of leadership development, we are here provided the chance to imagine leadership from four points of view expressed in this scholarship:

1. the leader—responsible for and accountable to the whole community the leader serves, and the external communities his or her enterprise is part of;

2. the community the leader serves;

3. the distinct, unique member of the community dependent upon the health of the community; and

4. the larger society that needs the communities within it to prosper.

The various contributions to this volume express and emphasize these points of view to reveal collectively a valuable tension among them that leads to the brilliance of the bridge metaphor for leadership studies: the contradictions and paradox in the concept of a dynamical system. We each express and contribute to these categories, often at the same time. We play leadership roles ourselves, we play contributing roles within the community, we are members of the community, and we comprise the global society the communities serve. Society depends upon communities, from family and education and work to infrastructure and governance; each of these is comprised of disparate elements.

For example, "Facilitating Sustainable Community Leadership Development: The Mid-South Delta Leaders Program Approach" by Lovell, Tabb, and Montesi (see pages 14–26), presents research showing that leadership development programs must focus on the personal skills and knowledge of the individual in order to produce outcomes of a shared future and purpose and community engagement. It would seem counterintuitive that development of one's personal skills is necessary for an outcome of a vision of a shared future and a stronger and more conscious community. At the same time, the authors maintain that "programs that are intended to address community issues must go beyond individual development in order to increase the capacity of a community to work together to address complex issues." How do we reconcile the contradiction of personal and community, individual goals and a common future? Similarly, in "Initial Thoughts about Competition and the Sustainability of Leadership" (see pages 27–36), Rechtman argues that the very values and virtues that can lead to one's becoming a leader, the ability to collaborate and cooperate in cohorts, are then replaced by the necessity to promote competition, leadership which is "ironically . . . a result of their own efforts to build cohesion." These are examples of the paradoxes that exist for leadership when an individual is both a member of a group and of many groups, and at the same time a member of a community, and set of communities, each with a different set of goals and values.

In reading these articles together as one piece, images formed in my mind that build on these paradoxes illuminating how any community by definition contains a diversity of roles and entities simultaneously.

 THE VARIOUS CONTRIBUTIONS TO THIS VOLUME . . . REVEAL COLLECTIVELY A VALUABLE TENSION AMONG THEM THAT LEADS TO THE BRILLIANCE OF THE BRIDGE METAPHOR FOR LEADERSHIP STUDIES.

Baseball and the Paradox of Community

There are, to begin with, two teams, and in opposition to each other. Together, they do not cancel each other out, or undermine the whole; rather, they make up part of the "whole" that is the game of baseball itself, which also includes other support units: umpires, "batboys" (bat-staff?), managers, and coaches. Each of them in turn is comprised of members who have individual and distinct roles (first base, pitcher, catcher, right fielder, shortstop, and so on). An individual member of a team will play offense and defense, in turn. The community organizes resources and policies around the game of baseball, and in the U.S., the game has the stature and value of "the national past-time." Society at large is invested in baseball, from the marketing of the sponsors, the development of equipment, the organization within schools of leagues and teams that are part of children's development, and even the language that informs how political, labor, educational, media, and other sectors talk (people who never see a game will say, "she threw me a curve," "you're batting 1000!" or "three strikes and you're out").

But baseball is also a wonderful image of the paradox of community for an additional reason. Here we see a game in which—at the same time—an individual and a community engage. The batter represents the individual in the community, acting alone (albeit encouraged and advised by team coaches and spectators—or not). But in the next inning, this same person is now part of a team, playing a specific role, one different from every other person on the team, part of an enterprise in which all are engaged in a common purpose: to get the batter "out." Meanwhile, at the same time, the lone individual has a purpose on behalf of her or his team—to "get home." Thus the "whole" of the game has several competing and contradictory goals at the same time—those of the team whose batter is on home plate, those of the team who are in the field, those of members in the outfield intent on catching the fly ball and making an "out," those of people on the bases with the responsibility of fielding the ball ahead of the runner, and so on. Scoring depends on the ability of the batters and runners to withstand the cooperation and collaboration of the team in the field to eliminate them from the action. Baseball as a conceptual whole is defined by the simultaneous interaction of coexisting entities, individual and community in a strict and ordered balance, the exchanging of roles as individual and community, and each member expressing a different location, skill, goal, and point of view. Even in the position of leader, people take turns: catcher, calling the pitch; pitcher, catching the ball and deciding the immediate strategy for fielding it (throw to third? throw to first? run to home plate and tag the runner trying to get home?). In this game, you could say that whoever has the ball is for that moment the leader, influencing and determining the action of everyone else; and everyone is a member of the team, and the game as a whole. One cannot be effective in his or her role unless one knows the purpose and ability and role of every other person on the field.

This metaphor supports the logic of the seeming paradoxes our authors illuminate—for example, in the Mid-South Delta Leaders Program by authors Lovell, Tabb, and Montesi. As noted by Rechtman, leadership demands both collaborative skills and the ability to mobilize the organization for intense competition; these skills are not either/or, but, as in the game of baseball as a whole, seemingly oppositional elements and qualities coexist and interact simultaneously. Referring to Robert Putnam's *Bowling Alone*, in which the concept of social capital is defined in terms of the ability to foster connections, Rechtman says, "the creation of bridging and bonding social capital enacts the opposite instrumentalities of conflict and collaboration in the leader's approach." As in baseball, two teams interact, one represented by individual players who set out from home one at a time, and one represented by a set of differently skilled players who cooperate; and both teams serve a greater collective purpose.

The Constitution: Where the Paradox of Community Is Worked Out

Another image that comes to mind in considering the paradoxes invoked by the research studies is the Constitution of the United States, which balances the needs and rights of the Individual and those of the Community. In this structure, the Preamble discusses the needs of "we the people," the good of the whole, the common futures. The Bill of Rights at the end discusses particular and would-be competing interests of individuals and individual groups.

The diversity between individuals and entities within systems that seems oppositional yet serves the greater whole is a principle feature of Culham's work on "The Leader's Role in Cultivating Intuition in the Workplace" (see pages 37–45). We see a poignant example of the challenge and opportunity of diversity in the organizational environment through the lens of a psychological insight into different ways people process and respond to information. One "minority group" is highlighted.

Culham discusses the fate within an organization of the person who is "intuitive" in a sea of "sensing types"—types identified by tests which help people understand their approaches to decision making and participation in groups. Intuitives bring up new possibilities and new solutions. Culham recognizes both a group (intuitive types) and the value of behavior that seem very much in the minority. He wants us to see how related are the two issues, and, to my mind, draws an exciting parallel to Einstein when he quotes, "We have created a society that honors the servant and has forgotten the gift." It is Einstein, after all, who created the cognitive and equally counterintuitive bridge of his famous formulation, $e=mc^2$. Similarly, the question of how seeming opposites coexist frames Pelletier's argument concerning ethics and transformational leadership: are ethical leaders transformational or are transformational leaders ethical? (See her chapter on pages 46–59.) The way Pelletier constructs the literature review brings to mind not only the analogies of baseball and the U.S. Constitution, but the circumstance of any dynamical system comprised of seeming opposite forces in ceaseless interplay.

If an approach is useful, as Culham suggests, such as intuitive types bringing new possibilities to the workplace, why would such types and approaches not be valued? It could be, paradoxically and also in terms of common sense, that a person who comes up with new possibilities is not really popular, and is, in fact, seen as a troublemaker, because the person is actually introducing a disturbance, a perturbation, and turbulence into the situation. We are now in the language of chaos theory, which explains the phenomena of new energy entering any dynamical system. The relevance of chaos theory to the workplace and leadership challenges and mandates is not coincidental.

The Butterfly and the Paradox of Individual Responsibility for a Sustainable Community

The paradox of organizational behavior, in which diverse elements coexist within one system, is that dynamical systems are characterized by the interdependence of all units. This is a behavioral principle of dynamical organizations. Because the members or units of an organization ("the whole") are seen to belong together as a functional entity, the behavior of one affects the behavior of all. The science which describes these relationships in dynamical systems is chaos and complexity theories, originating in physics and mathematics. The theories describe how things happen, basically how change occurs and activity is sustained in a dynamical system. Energy is cumulative and accrues in its impact. Referred to as the phenomenon whereby the interdependent system shows sensitivity to and dependence on internal motions, "the butterfly effect" takes its name from the idea that a butterfly flapping its wings in Brazil causes a storm system in Texas. Something considered small in one place, an "initial factor," over time and space this action can become momentous, because the energy systems are all interrelated and build on one another. Energy bridges already exist.

The implications for leaders and leadership studies are illuminated in this "bridges" approach to leadership scholarship. We see that Pelletier relates ethical decision making to a process within a system in which "unethical decision making creates invisible barriers that hinder the organic functioning of an organization, and if unchecked, could lead to entropy." Thus leaders do not only bear responsibility for a vision of the organization as a whole which creates bridges among the units (thereby ensuring behavioral models of a dynamical system), but maintenance of the individual units which each play a pivotal role in the overall functioning of the organization. Moreover, dynamical system behavior enables a leader more accurately and productively to gauge progress over time. If something that appears initially to be small can actually be growing into something powerful over time, leaders can develop a long-term approach to assessment. In the Mid-South Delta Leaders Program described by Lovell, Tabb, and Montesi, for example, we see the conclusion that "it is important to note that initiatives such as [the program] are often difficult to evaluate due to not only the intangible nature of many of the outcomes, but also the longer time frame necessary to see 'community change.' But, as one program participant stated, 'we may not see the impact [the program] has on the region immediately, but I think each of us is trying to make inroads into the places where we work, volunteer, where we do business, and where we educate our children. I think the results of our training will help others get involved in a way that will make a difference. I find myself reaching out and bridging to new people who can help change some of the negatives that abound in our region."

For program leaders such as at Mid-South Delta, therefore, it is important to develop an assessment tool that factors in the long-range behavior of systems. People can give up on worthwhile projects because we are looking for evidence of success too early. In fact, what chaos theory reveals about dynamical systems is that whatever is set in motion initially causes disturbances or perturbations, a turbulence that eventually "self organizes" into patterns of coherence and overall order. Knowledge of how systems work is critical to developing not only the plans but also the assessment strategies for those plans when they are implemented. The exciting aspect of the Leaders Program at Mid-South Delta is that it is incorporating into the leadership development program the concepts of chaos theory in ways that promote morale and ensure the sustainability of the project.

This way of thinking is what I would call "the power of the butterfly." It is the understanding within an organization that one's own efforts, however humble and small they may appear, especially compared to the enormity of problems and challenges the organization faces, can be significant. To foster this understanding is one of the most critical accomplishments for long-term success for a leader or a leadership development program. Contributors to the mission can feel more valued and encouraged by a long-term view of projected outcomes. The long-term view of any dynamical system builds morale, and promotes the sustainability of the enterprise. Here we see an inspiring example of how leadership program participants express a faith in what is essentially chaos theory—the long, long view. The story of the Mid-South Delta program reminds us of the role of hope that leadership can generate: it is fundamental to a proactive effort to achieve a goal.

 WHAT CHAOS THEORY REVEALS ABOUT DYNAMICAL SYSTEMS IS THAT WHATEVER IS SET IN MOTION INITIALLY CAUSES DISTURBANCES OR PERTURBATIONS, A TURBULENCE THAT EVENTUALLY "SELF ORGANIZES" INTO PATTERNS OF COHERENCE AND OVERALL ORDER.

Klamon makes the paradigm of chaos theory explicit in her work that connects leadership and organizational stability, specifically in service of a whole in which the bottom line serves social good (see pages 60–77). In the whole systems paradigm, the concept of competition is inherently impractical for long-term goals. Klamon's conviction that an emerging form of entrepreneurial organization will be a social enterprise rather than what I imagine is a more short-term approach she terms the "capitalism paradigm." Klamon's essay is invigorated with the language of chaos and systems theory. Focusing on the servant leadership model, Klamon urges an approach which will create a "healthy, sustainable workplace." Toward this end there is a recognition of the dynamics of the workplace that include responsiveness to top-down management, even "heartfelt" vision when it is dictated. As Klamon quotes Wheatley, "The command and control model of leadership inhibits people from working together in meaningful ways and is out of step with the requirements of our evolving world marketplace." Similarly, our Finnish colleague in the collection, Maijastiina Rouhiainen, calls for a "leadership dialogue." Rouhiainen (see pages 78–92) promotes a new perspective on the interpersonal factors which lie at the core of leadership. Calling for a more philosophical approach to leadership, in which any dialogue becomes multi-dimensional and exists in a complex social construction, we are back to complexity and whole systems theories, cross-cultural bridging, and interaction in a world that is interdependent. This is further supported by Salter et al. (see pages 93–106) in their consideration of "transformational leaders as highly differentiated communicators who meet the implicit expectations of followers with their communications." Again and again in this volume is vibrant testimony to the conviction that what the workplace needs now is "participative competence," collaborative and cooperative interaction across sectors that is at the heart of bridging and the nexus of whole systems theories.

Chaos theory informs essays on the humanities and literature as well. Provizer's essay (see pages 107–117) cites Tolstoy who sees reality resting on multiple causation, saying "the more 'we delve in search of these causes the more of them we find; and each separate cause or whole series of causes appears to us equally valid in itself and equally false by its insignificance compared to the magnitude of the events.'" In this round world of system dynamics, multiple truths coexist. We see chaos theory in Provizer's analysis of the leader's reality: no leader can control events—even the "greatest king was only 'history's slave'"—as Provizer quotes James McGregor Burns. Leaders deal with events beyond their own and their society's comprehension (he cites Lincoln's assertion that he does not control events; rather, events control him). I find myself reflecting how fascinating it would be to apply the scholarship of this volume's insights as advice to Lincoln and other leaders, who would find practicality as well as solace in the interweaving wisdom of humanities and sciences for morale-building reinforcement of long-term strategies.

In our time machine, we could "bridge" the lessons on leadership from emergent scholarship to leaders on the field and in the field. That, I hope, is a way this volume on bridges can serve the current field of leadership studies. Although the individuals and teams reporting on their scholarship on leadership appear to have very different approaches and foci, there are strong connections invoked by the concept of "bridges." In the deep structure of this volume, we see data and evidence for long-term healthy communities and organizations promoting and developing ways for people and their ideas to connect minds, hearts, conscience, and consciousness. There is humanity and heart in these essays, and on that note, I will close with thoughts about two essays that combine arts and science.

The team of Edwards, Turnbull, Stephens, and Johnston (see pages 118–133) emphasize the word "integrating" in setting out a topic about sustainability thinking and practice. Sumantra Ghoshal is cited for ideas about management practices that promote sustainable development that require a change in the mind-set and values of society's leaders—which the British team feels could happen in higher education's leadership programs, such as a master's course. Such a program would build leaders' abilities to forge relationships within and between functions. Sustainability, a key application of chaos theory to organizations, is also part of Redekop's "Leading into a Sustainable Future" (see pages 134–146). He concludes with an image of the sustainable leader as a storyteller and image-maker. Citing (once again) the "complex, multifaceted" aspects of leadership, Redekop argues that leaders' abilities to inspire change is part of a mutual process of shaping images of reality, what we can see as a chaotic process of influence based on interdependence. The leader who can tell a "springboard" story connecting a past achievement with a future achievement is indeed an engineer of bridge work, helping people get over a natural resistance to change and fear of adversity. In a wonderful quote from Harter, Redekop emphasizes, "Leadership is the process by which one person exposes and replaces the fallacy of misplaced concreteness, enabling others to gain separation from their preexisting mental constructs—of themselves, each other, their social context, and possible futures—so that we might all see things anew, nearer in fact to the reality where ultimately we wish to flourish." This bridge work seems foundational to the calls throughout this volume for greater interaction and communication among leaders and members of the communities the leader serves.

What is at stake in such bridge work? Redekop makes a heart-felt conclusion: "In this and other ways—many yet to be conceived—we can begin to understand how we as leaders and followers can help bring into being a world that lasts." It is clear that writers in the leadership field are concerned with social outcomes on a great and long-term scale. Leadership itself is believed to matter for society's survival. Thus we all have a great stake in how we support and educate leaders. Whether we look at the realities for which leaders can be prepared in terms of science, or arts, or even baseball and the Constitution, we find that the greater a leader's ability to envision the reality that governs a community or organization, the more flexible, creative, resourceful, useful, long term, and successful a leader will be. Our authors stress that the reality of human systems requires most of all an understanding of the human interactivity that exists and can be supported and promoted. In this sense, leadership development is engineering training, bridge-making, the facilitation of connection, so that everyone in the community, including the leader, can be a "butterfly." We can each believe in our own and each other's capacity to make a difference because of the bridges that exist, the interdependence that is the bottom line of any dynamical system. In this case, the poet Robert Frost is right—"Something there is that does not love a wall," and that something is our own feisty survival instinct aware that it is in making better bridges that we will provide sustainable infrastructure to be useful and noble in our lives.

DR. BARBARA MOSSBERG is President Emerita of Goddard College. She currently is a Senior Scholar at the James McGregor Burns Academy of Leadership at the University of Maryland and serves as Director and Professor of Integrated Studies at California State University Monterey Bay.

Facilitating Sustainable Community Leadership Development

The Mid-South Delta Leaders Program Approach

By Donielle M. Lovell, Myrtis Tabb, and Christy Montesi

TREMENDOUS AMOUNTS OF RESOURCES ARE FILTERED INTO community leadership development within the United States. Over the last decade, these programs increased in number, due in part to the changing social environments in communities (Langone & Rohs, 1995). Such programs are seen as one method to address the necessary capacity building needed by community leaders to effectively lead and create solutions for community problems—including those felt by rural communities in terms of globalization. The outcomes of globalization are reinterpreted on the local level where "individuals attempt to make sense of situations and construct their daily life through interpretations of these situations" (Kleiner, 2005). To some degree, it is community leaders who must interpret the situations and facilitate the interaction needed to respond and adapt to challenges.

The intent of most leadership development programs is to enable leaders to work with groups in meaningful ways, build the capacity of individuals to problem solve, and orientate leaders to a learning approach that anticipates change rather than reacts to shock changes in their environment (Botkin, Elmandjra, & Malitza, 1979; Day, 2000). According to Day, leadership development can also be conceptualized as an integration strategy by "helping people understand how to relate to others, coordinate their efforts, build commitments and develop extended social networks" (2000, p. 586).

Furthermore, as discussed by Bridger and Alter (2006), the work of these programs must address not only personal skills that can be used in various outlets (i.e., career development), but must also provide strategies for improving the capacity of a community to act. They suggest programs include models of community action and facilitate interactions among participants that address community building as well as individual skill development. Programs that focus on these components within the cultural context of the community can provide a sustainable means of not only providing the necessary skills for community change, but also sustainable methods of facilitating action and interaction within the locale.

 THE INTENT OF MOST LEADERSHIP DEVELOPMENT PROGRAMS IS TO ENABLE LEADERS TO WORK WITH GROUPS IN MEANINGFUL WAYS, BUILD THE CAPACITY OF INDIVIDUALS TO PROBLEM SOLVE, AND ORIENTATE LEADERS TO A LEARNING APPROACH THAT ANTICIPATES CHANGE RATHER THAN REACTS TO SHOCK CHANGES IN THEIR ENVIRONMENT.

This paper addresses one such approach to community leadership development—the Mid-South Delta Leaders (MSDL) Program. The approach of the program is discussed here as well as results from various evaluation activities over a three-year period focusing on two classes of the MSDL program. Evaluation results address the importance of creating leadership programs that develop the individual leader as well as provide the necessary tools for community development and interaction.

Communities of Place and Leadership

As Bridger and Alter (2006) point out, the death of the notion of place-based community is a popular topic in sociological literature. And, given the impact of economic globalization on the rural community, researchers argue the concept of the place-based community is further damaged. Theories such as the "Great Change" (Warren, 1978) point out the difficulty of community as place in a global society. Warren argued that community is nothing more than the "stage where extra-local groups, organizations, and businesses pursued their interests with little concern for how their actions affected local residents" (Luloff & Bridger, 2003, p. 205). This notion continues with the discussion of globalization and the increase in technological communications.

However, these larger global processes have not nullified community as place, but rather they have reshaped elements such as structure and culture within a community. The local, place-based community will always affect material, social, and mental well-being of residents in important ways (Luloff & Bridger, 2003). The major constant in defining community and making the concept and practice of community development sustainable is interaction. By placing community in an interactional framework, it allows one to acknowledge the changes that have taken place in the modern community in that they are not the integrated unit of the past, while still remembering citizens in a common locale will interact to address issues that have impact on their lives (Luloff & Bridger, 2003).

Since interaction is an essential element of community, development activities must build the capacity for interaction or collaboration among its citizens. Instead of beginning development efforts by pointing out the deficiencies of the community, it is useful and sustainable to start from the one persistent element of community— interaction. How does a community act as it goes about solving problems?

Community leadership programs must operate within the appropriate historical, social, and cultural framework of the community. These aspects influence the interaction among residents. When considering the design of the program, facilitators must consider the issues surrounding the community or region as they decide how to best approach capacity-building exercises.

Leadership Development in the Mississippi Delta

The Mid-South Delta Leaders Program is an eighteen-month leadership development program aimed at enhancing the skills of leaders in the 55-county/parish Delta region of Arkansas, Louisiana, and Mississippi and funded by the W. K. Kellogg Foundation. MSDL uses an innovative approach to enhance the skills of promising Delta leaders. This program is aimed at increasing the intellectual capital in the tri-state Delta region to create a positive future for the area. Deltans from all sectors get to know and work with one another through the MSDL curriculum that uses a variety of exercises and experiences to coach members in the development of a global perspective. It is the expected outcome of MSDL that a generation of leaders will emerge who appreciate the value of well-calculated risks and creating innovative, creative, persistent and strong partnerships across sectors.

MSDL helps to further develop the class members' understanding of three major systems: education, public policy formation, and economic. Each is influenced in the Delta by historical, social, and cultural traditions. New understandings, based on critical analysis, help to enhance the development of participant competencies to work with other citizens in organizational and community settings as a means of effectively bringing about desired changes for the good of the Delta region. The Delta cannot compete effectively in the emerging global economic system if it does not develop better understandings of its heritage and the lingering human relations issues. The unique history and heritage of the Delta must be understood and taken into account as development programs are planned. Community pride fosters collaboration as citizens work toward positive change.

The future of the Delta's socioeconomic well-being is irrevocably intertwined with issues of cross-cultural understanding, human relations, and its public policy, economic, and educational systems. Deltans and the nation have tried programs that seek to address the issues. As Cobb (1992) suggests in his book, *The Most Southern Place on Earth*, the Delta must look outward to ways of the world in learning how to solve problems in its own society. Simply putting money into the Delta, however, has not and will not work without improving the understanding of, and in some cases overcoming, some aspects of the Delta's complex heritage. Therefore, the designers of this program recognize that, in providing a leadership development experience, the interaction of the participants is key to the overall success of not only the program process, but in what the participants will be able to facilitate within their own community.

 SIMPLY PUTTING MONEY INTO THE DELTA HAS NOT AND WILL NOT WORK WITHOUT IMPROVING THE UNDERSTANDING OF, AND IN SOME CASES OVERCOMING, SOME ASPECTS OF THE DELTA'S COMPLEX HERITAGE.

Program Curriculum and Strategy

The Mid-South Delta Leaders Program curriculum is based on an earlier initiative that involved only the eighteen-county region of the Mississippi Delta—the Delta Emerging Leaders Program. The MSDL strategy is driven by a four-fold belief about leaders and leadership. First, leaders must know what they are talking about to be effective leaders. Second, they must understand the broader picture in which productive change happens. Therefore, it is the intent of the program to educate leaders from not only a local and regional perspective, but also from a global perspective. Third, a leader must plan well. The program equips leaders with effective community and economic development techniques as well as ways to facilitate discussion to help plan meaningful change. Finally, it is the belief of MSDL that leaders must execute boldly. The MSDL class members plan and implement a symposium based upon their experience and learning. Beyond the context of the program, the expectation of bold execution shows in the action and interaction in which participants engage in their home community in order to facilitate change.

MSDL class members work together through an eighteen-month process of stimulating dialogue, idea sharing, study travel tours, learning retreats, and other educational experiences. This multifaceted approach is invaluable for participants in their quests to understand and develop comprehensive strategies to approach the complex issues and challenges facing the Delta region. The program helps develop human resources, which in turn will allow Delta communities to help themselves. The MSDL curriculum is designed to help leaders on an individual level develop the competencies mentioned earlier through:

- guiding leaders in improving their leadership, management, and communication skills;
- assisting leaders in gaining a deeper understanding and appreciation of the Delta's socioeconomic and cultural realities;
- equipping leaders with a better understanding of national and global trends and how they influence the quality of life and community development in the tri-state Delta;
- helping leaders build local and regional partnerships to create and manage change in their communities;
- recognizing how to influence policy and programmatic initiatives in cross-cultural and diverse socioeconomic settings;
- linking leaders with other educational programs and action strategies; and,
- empowering leaders to increase their involvement in community and economic development efforts locally.

The Mid-South Delta Leaders Program uses a variety of learning methods to meet its goals. Four learning retreats are directed toward different aspects of leadership development. These three-day events consist of workshops led by participants, consultants, and program staff. The retreats introduce participants to new areas of knowledge, provide a context for positive working relationships with other participants, and enhance participants' skills in a variety of leadership behaviors. Next, participants use the "Delta Connection," an Internet-based peer learning approach to maintain interaction and contact in the months between face-to-face meetings. Two study travel tours are arranged for MSDL participants. One study tour focuses on public policy and the role of government at the state level, and the second provides a firsthand view of the tri-state Delta region. Finally, MSDL class members bring their own wealth of networking resources to the table. Therefore, they mobilize these networks along with the new resources gained in the program to plan a tri-state event to explore opportunities for action in the Delta. The activities engaged in by participants build their skills and capacity for engagement and interaction within their home community.

Evaluation Framework

There are a number of possible solutions as to the best evaluation model for initiatives such as the one just described. The MSDL evaluation framework consists of traditional evaluation approaches combined with empowerment evaluation tools and action research. This method is important because it focuses on participant involvement in evaluating development ventures (Fetterman, Kaftarian, & Wandersman, 1996; Harley, Stebnicki, & Rollins, 2000). Qualitative interviews, focus groups, participant observation, and a pre/posttest are used to evaluate this effort.

The evaluation includes a partnership between the researcher and MSDL program staff who are instrumental in the success of communicating with the participants about the importance of this evaluation research. Furthermore, the intent of the evaluation process is to include important parties, such as the staff, in the activities. Since the evaluation is an ongoing part of the program, the continual cycle of feedback from program participants to program staff is important in continuing the certain evolution of the program.

Qualitative interviews were conducted with class members to ascertain the context in which they operate as leaders. The pre-interviews provide information as to how they currently view their leadership activities and what impacts they anticipate involvement in MSDL will bring. The post-interview process provides details as to how the MSDL program content has influenced their leadership skills and knowledge, their networks, and their resolve to lead within the Delta. It also explores the context in which these leaders are using their skills, resources, and networks obtained during the course of the program. Interview information provided in this paper is derived from Class I and II.

Focus groups were conducted at two different times during the evaluation process. A midpoint focus group explored the participants' experience within the program to that point, allowing them to make known issues to be discussed or content to be reviewed. A second focus group was conducted near the end of the program to explore what next steps are needed in terms of their leadership involvement in the tri-state Delta once they have finished the program. It also provided an opportunity to discuss how they may utilize the networks created during the course of the program. It is yet another opportunity to provide feedback for the continual improvement of the program. The findings from the interviews and focus groups are described below.

Evaluation Findings

One hundred twenty-nine Delta residents have participated in MSDL since 2004. Table 1 provides the demographics for the participants.

Table 1: Demographics of MSDL Class I and II participants

Gender		Ethnicity	
Male	50	African American	80
Female	79	Caucasian	48
		Other	1
Employment Sector		**Age**	
Higher Education	20	20–29	16
K–12 Education	12	30–39	42
Volunteer	4	40–49	34
For Profit	23	50–59	28
Nonprofit	41	60–69	8
Local Government	20	70–79	1
Faith-Based	4		
Health	5		

Participants were very positive in their discussion of the skills and knowledge gained through the MSDL curriculum. As one Mississippi member shared,

Last year, I was elected President of our Chamber of Commerce. Over the past year, many issues have come before me. Some have dealt with economic development while others have been issues of personality. MSDL has taught me how to deal with conflicts that occur in a leadership role.

Class members also commented on the knowledge they gained about the Delta as a whole. Many reflected that they thought they knew the region since they were lifelong residents, but realized after the program there was more to the story of the Delta. A member of Class I reflected upon this aspect after deciding to enroll in a PhD program in Heritage Studies:

I selected the Heritage Studies program after MSDL exposed me to the great diversity of culture and history in the Delta. I had a reawakening of my educational needs during MSDL. Through my contacts in MSDL, I discovered this PhD program and decided to return to school.

In terms of interaction stimulated by the program, participants discussed both the networks created among the class members as well as those skills that enabled them to facilitate action in a community. Throughout the evaluation processes, participants frequently discuss the enlargement of their personal networks as an important outcome of the MSDL program. As one individual stated,

> There are people that I've met through MSDL that I will never forget, but more importantly the depth of each developed relationship will lend to an even broader network. It's not always who you know, but who they know.

Another participant reflected,

> I have gained new relationships that will foster change in our communities. I have seen different parts of our region and met people that I might have otherwise never experienced in my lifetime.

However, many may wonder how and if these networks are utilized by the participants. While there are numerous examples from this endeavor, those cited below are indicative of the kind of interaction participants engaged in following their MSDL experience.

In one of the classes, a group from the same town had not met prior to involvement with MSDL. During their carpool to one of the retreats they discussed the political situation in their town including the upcoming mayoral elections. Conversation turned to the lack of information on the various candidates running for office. They were concerned about this lack and how it might influence the ability of citizens to make an informed decision. Therefore, in cooperation with several local organizations, they organized a public debate, which was attended by over 350 community members (Mid-South Delta Initiative Newsletter, 2004). This is the kind of community action a leadership program hopes to encourage.

Even leaders who have a long record of public service discussed the ways in which they have utilized the action strategies talked about in MSDL. As one member stated,

> I have been involved in public service for eighteen years. Since my involvement with MSDL, I've started a coalition of other leaders to sit down at the table, share

our common goals, and work together toward those goals. In other words, it's not just me doing it myself. I have become more inclusive.

Another long time Delta activist stated,

> I have a new excitement about what I do. I have been a volunteer and professional for many years. I think you can burn out or get stale in your thinking. MSDL renewed my faith in the people of my region, my love for my region and heritage, and my hope for the future. It was a great rebirth for me.

Participants often discussed the empowering experience of MSDL and how that can in turn influence their communities. As one individual stated,

> Empowering people with the skills to improve their lives and influencing their attitudes through education and personal contact has been one of my goals since I became involved with MSDL.

> I never thought I would be in a classroom with so many other people that shared the same ideas and concerns that I had and were willing to put their beliefs and differences aside and find common ground or the middle of the road and work toward these goals.

Part of MSDL is class members mobilizing their resources. Class II members organized a Delta-wide summit entitled "Delta WISE…Working to Influence the Spirit of Entente." The focus of this meeting was to compare and contrast the efforts of Arkansas, Louisiana, and Mississippi in education, economic development, and public policy. The event also focused on the assets of the region that can be used to promote community and economic development. Class members brought together elected officials, organizations, and community residents. The audience was invited to hear the panelists, but it was also an interactive event to stimulate conversation about the region among the 125 participants.

A Little Can Go a Long Way
Graduates can apply for community development seed money following the completion of the program. Many graduates applied for money on their own, but some collaborated on a project. Twelve projects are currently in different stages of development, though only three are shared here.

One graduate used the seed money to help in the development of a local farmers market. This was not strictly an MSDL funded project. The community had already collaborated on many aspects, but like many projects just needed some extra funding. Grand opening was held in the Spring of 2005. The class member reports that the event was a huge success. Not only did they have vendors selling their produce, but also ball teams with baked goods, live music, health screenings, a state park interpreter with an alligator, and many more events. She also reports that the market pavilion has become a local gathering spot with organizations using the area for bake sales and other community events. Furthermore, she is working to expand the market by recruiting farmers from neighboring counties to participate. Other class members are also aiding in this effort by passing the word along to their local farmers.

 EVEN LEADERS WHO HAVE A LONG RECORD OF PUBLIC SERVICE DISCUSSED THE WAYS IN WHICH THEY HAVE UTILIZED THE ACTION STRATEGIES TALKED ABOUT IN MSDL.

A second project, a nonprofit organization called Vision for the Future, was established with the available funds. This organization provides small academic scholarships for local high school students. During 2006 the first scholarships were given to two students. This organization also speaks to high school groups about the importance of higher education and other scholarship opportunities as information is often lacking in theses small, rural communities.

Finally, four class members established "Delta Leaders Innovating Community Collaborations (Delta LINCCS). This organization seeks to provide Delta nonprofits with seed money to aid in capacity building. In January 2006 the organization provided a small amount of funds to seven organizations ranging from a local school reading program to a church after-school program.

Discussion

Through the implementation of the MSDL curriculum, participants received leadership skills training that contributed to their professional and personal growth. Leaders are then sharing that knowledge with others in their community. These participants are using the capacity-building skills developed in MSDL to participate in community and economic development initiatives. The program staff believes that the growth, knowledge, and skills of all MSDL participants will be sustainable. Networks, connections, and relationships developed through the program will be long term. Once developed, linkages and leadership skills can never be withdrawn.

MSDL is developing a spirit of volunteerism and service in its staff, participants, partners, and local citizens. Many may argue that leadership development programs that are funded like MSDL, through foundations, are not sustainable because once funding ceases so does the program. MSDL program staff argues this is not necessarily true. The spirit of the program lives beyond funding cycles. The outcomes of MSDL will continue to have an impact on the lives of citizens in low resource Delta communities. Strengthening leadership skills provides opportunities for community and economic development, and the investment of MSDL in its participants and others will continue to improve the conditions of the Delta and ensure sustainability.

> **"** **MSDL IS DEVELOPING A SPIRIT OF VOLUNTEERISM** **"**
> **AND SERVICE IN ITS STAFF, PARTICIPANTS,**
> **PARTNERS, AND LOCAL CITIZENS.**

The Mid-South Delta Leaders Program could be easily replicated in other rural regions of the country. MSDL is creating a network of leaders in the tri-state Delta who are willing and able to work together for the betterment of their region. A regional leadership development initiative, such as MSDL, could act as a catalyst for momentum of providing technical assistance and support to communities throughout rural America. This, in turn, increases the breadth and depth of networks, and ensures the inclusion of stakeholders, particularly those traditionally underrepresented in community and economic development efforts. By adapting the MSDL model, other areas would be able to strengthen their collaborative (interactional) leadership base through a formal, structured approach.

Results of our work indicate that leadership development programs must focus on the personal skills and knowledge of the individual in order to produce outcomes such as a shared future and purpose as well as civic engagement. Community leadership development work must address the interaction aspect of the community and provide opportunities for participants to learn, grow, and serve in this arena. Community of place has not disappeared—people still structure their lives around the institutions in communities. It is in these places they educate their children and work. Therefore, programs that are intended to address community issues must go beyond individual development in order to increase the capacity of a community to work together to address complex issues.

Finally, it is important to note that initiatives such as MSDL are often difficult to evaluate due not only to the intangible nature of many of the outcomes, but also the longer time frame necessary to see "community change." But, as one program participant stated,

We may not see the impact MSDL has on the region immediately, but I think each of us is trying to make inroads into the places where we work, volunteer, where we do business, and where we educate our children. I think the results of our training will help others get involved in a way that will make a difference. I find myself reaching out and bridging to new people who can help change some of the negatives that abound in our region.

REFERENCES

Botkin, J. W., Elmandjra, M., & Malitza, M. (1979). *No limits to learning: Bridging the human gap.* Oxford: Pergamon Press.

Bridger, J. C., & Alter, T. R. (2006). Place, community development and social capital. *Journal of the Community Development Society, 37*, 5–18.

Cobb, J. C. (1992). *The most southern place on Earth: The Mississippi Delta and the roots of regional identity.* New York: Oxford University Press.

Day, D. V. (2000). Leadership development: A review in context. *Leadership Quarterly, 11*(4), 581–613.

Fetterman, D. M., Kaftarian, S. J., & Wandersman, A. (Eds.). (1996). *Empowerment evaluation: Knowledge and tools for self-assessment and accountability.* Thousand Oaks, CA: Sage Publications.

Harley, D., Stebnicki, A. M., & Rollins, C. W. (2000). Applying empowerment evaluation as a tool for self-improvement and community development with culturally diverse populations. *Journal of the Community Development Society, 31*, 348–364.

Kleiner, A. (2005). *Achieving social change through community-based research: An analysis of participatory research approaches.* Presentation to COD 695: Needs Assessment, Asset Mapping, and Evaluation. Graduate course at Delta State University.

Langone, C. A., & Rohs, F. R. (1995). Community leadership development: Process and practice. *Journal of the Community Development Society, 26*, 252–267.

Luloff, A. E., & Bridger, J. C. (2003). Community agency and local development. In D. L. Brown & L. E. Swanson (Eds.), *Challenges for rural America in the twenty-first century.* University Park: The University of Pennsylvania.

Mid-South Delta Initiative Newsletter. (2004). Local leaders unite Delta community to organize political forum. Retrieved April 28, 2007, from http://msdi.org/newsletters/archive/deltalinksNOV2004.pdf

Warren, R. L. (1978). *The community in America* (3rd ed.). Chicago: Rand McNally.

DONIELLE LOVELL is a PhD candidate in the department of rural sociology at the University of Missouri. She earned an MS in community development from Delta State University. She has worked on various leadership initiatives in the Mississippi Delta for five years. Her current work focuses on the impact of Delta culture on leadership attainment and attitudes.

MYRTIS TABB, Assistant Vice President for Partnerships and Special Projects and Tri-State Leader of the Mid-South Delta Leaders at Delta State University, has more than twenty-five years of professional experience in education, leadership and community development. She was instrumental in the conceptualization, development, and implementation of the Mid-South Delta Leaders Program and the Delta Emerging Leaders Program. A native of Mississippi, she earned the EdD in educational administration at Delta State University.

CHRISTY MONTESI serves as the Assistant Director of the Office of Special Projects and the Tri-State Director of the Mid-South Delta Leaders Program. She has twelve years of professional experience in community and leadership development. A native of the Mississippi Delta, she earned a Master of Science in Community Development and a Master of Business Administration from Delta State University.

Initial Thoughts about Competition and the Sustainability of Leadership

By Janet E. Rechtman

The shadow is a moral problem that challenges the whole ego-personality, for no one can become conscious of the shadow without considerable moral effort. To become conscious of it involves recognizing the dark aspects of the personality as present and real. This act is the essential condition for any kind of self-knowledge.

Karl Jung (1951)

CONSIDER POLITICAL LEADERS. THEY COMPETE FOR ELECTED OFFICE. They compete for dollars in what National Public Radio (2007) has dubbed "the money primary," a race to raise the most money in an effort to "prove viability." Once in office, they raise competing ideas, seeking to win support from colleagues and voters in future campaigns. Surely the ability to compete is a key element of their leadership.

Consider business leaders. They compete to rise to positions of power and authority in companies. They build strategies that help their firms compete with other firms for market share. They motivate employees through internal competitions to meet goals, be the best team, or rise to positions of power and authority. Surely the ability to compete is a key element of their leadership.

Consider nonprofit and community leaders. Their missions compete against relentless diseases, disasters, and malign forces that seek to harm the world and its creatures. They compete with each other for the favor of government agencies and foundations as they seek contracts for service. Surely the ability to compete is a key element of their leadership.

Clearly, competition is a challenge inherent in the environment where leaders operate. Competition is also the capacity to mobilize adherents, promote visibility, and secure resources in the marketplace of ideas. Thus the ability to compete is a personal attribute making it possible for the individual to lead in the first place. This paper shares reflections, observations, and questions that have emerged in the author's thirty-plus years of practice as a leader and student of leadership in business and nonprofit settings. With more questions than answers and more provocation than resolution, it invites an intentional examination of a shadowy place where liberal thinkers are loath to tread. Over the last year, at least six of my nonprofit clients came to the following conclusion: "We have to learn how to compete like Republicans if we want to move our work forward." This paper ventures to reframe that conclusion, to say that leaders must learn more about what competition means before blindly adapting to a hostile environment.

> **" CLEARLY, COMPETITION IS A CHALLENGE INHERENT IN THE ENVIRONMENT WHERE LEADERS OPERATE. COMPETITION IS ALSO THE CAPACITY TO MOBILIZE ADHERENTS, PROMOTE VISIBILITY, AND SECURE RESOURCES IN THE MARKETPLACE OF IDEAS. "**

Competition Defined

In business, competition is most often an economic activity. Eighteenth-century moral philosopher Adam Smith (1776) postulated that firms seeking to market goods to consumers will encounter a host of similarly motivated marketers. Thus a system of natural liberty emerged, in which the iron hand of consumer demand, in the form of competition, imposed price disciplines on participants as they bid against each other for available customers. If any one individual or company strayed from the levels set for everyone, competition drove them back to the market level.

Such natural liberty was founded on the idea that economic freedom benefits the general public. "In a purely competitive market, the consumer is king," because they "enjoy goods that are produced as abundantly and sold as cheaply as possible . . . [and] each firm is producing the goods the consumer wants, in the largest quantities and at the lowest cost possible" (Heilbroner & Thurow, 1998, p. 166). In many cases, the situation of natural liberty is altered as firms use strategies such as advertising, barriers to exit and entry, and political advocacy to support prices that are higher than those that would naturally occur under perfect competition. In these cases, the consumer loses sovereignty. In economic terms, the state of natural liberty in which the consumer reigns supreme is known as *perfect competition*, and departures from this state are known as *imperfect competition*, or *structural competition*.

Outside of economics, competition is the enactment of a relationship among two or more individuals in which the parties strive for an asymmetrical outcome. The origins of the root word *compete* comes from the Latin *competere,* which rather benignly translates as to *seek together*. Over time this meaning has added connotations of mastery, disputes, and other aspects of conflict (Merriam-Webster, 2002). Thus the dictionary definition of competition as both rivalry and a joint endeavor conflates the opposing behaviors of conflict and collaboration.

This definition is borne out in practice. In sports, for example, two or more winning teams (a collaboration) engage in games (ritualized conflicts) governed by rules that are defined collaboratively. In business, leading competitors are companies whose teams (collaborations) enact conflicts with other companies to realize measurable gains in profitability or market share. In electoral politics, by the consent of the governed (a collaboration), leaders of collaboratives known as constituencies engage in public conflicts for votes, funds, and sound bites. In each of these cases, the parties engage in multiple intersecting dimensions of collaboration and conflict as they struggle toward an asymmetrical resolution. Leaders who excel in the process we call competition are comfortable enacting the *both-and* of conflict and collaboration. The open question is: Are people who are not so comfortable with conflict, collaboration, or the *both-and* blend of the two less likely or able to lead?

Competition among Leaders as the *Both-And* of Conflict and Collaboration

In the real worlds of politics, business, and community service, leaders must constantly and nimbly navigate between conflict and collaboration as they compete to mobilize followers, promote visibility, and secure resources. The outcome of this collection of activities is the Leader-Member Cohort (LMC), a term of art that plays on Northouse's Leader-Member eXchange (LMX) denomination (2001). I deliberately chose member instead of follower to signal that fairly strong but still voluntary barriers to exit and entry for participation. The word *cohort* is an apt description of the group that includes leader and followers, since the term originally denoted one of ten divisions of an ancient Roman legion (Merriam-Webster, 2002). The image of a group of warriors or soldiers captures the metaphorical and literal aspects of conflict and collaboration that is at the heart of competitive leadership.

The conflicts occur as the leader struggles to secure the visibility, adherents, and resources needed to sustain an LMC. When individuals reflect on their emergence as leaders, they tend to minimize competitive context, observing things like, "Someone asked me" or "No one else stepped up and I did" (Rechtman, 1997). This is because many LMCs first emerge when a formative cohort seeks to meet the needs of the initial adherents. Armed with the power of constituency, these same LMCs must now operate under conditions of structural competition that ironically may be a result of their own efforts to build cohesion.

66 **IN THE REAL WORLDS OF POLITICS, BUSINESS, AND COMMUNITY SERVICE, LEADERS MUST CONSTANTLY AND NIMBLY NAVIGATE BETWEEN CONFLICT AND COLLABORATION AS THEY COMPETE TO MOBILIZE FOLLOWERS, PROMOTE VISIBILITY, AND SECURE RESOURCES.** 99

At the same time as engaging in these conflicts, the leader must also foster collaboration within the LMC, to ensure consistency between in-group and out-of-group messages, the loyalty of new and experienced recruits, and wise deployment of resources. The outcome of this work is the creation of what Robert Putnam has called "bonding social capital" made up of networks, trust, and shared norms that promote reciprocity and solidarity within the LMC (Putnam, 2000, p. 22). Bonding social capital thus encourages cohort members to increase their loyalty to the LMC, effectively equipping the leader with a more competitive position in relation to other leaders. Further, even as these bonds are forming, the leader must also build "bridging social capital," a form of collaboration that supports linkage to external assets and facilitates communication with others (Putnam, 2000, p. 22). This bridging process enhances the credibility and visibility of the LMC in the broader community by creating and favorably resolving conflicts in the minds of those considering this among other options. Thus the creation of bridging and bonding social capital enacts the opposite instrumentalities of conflict and collaboration in the leader's approach.

Leadership Is a Form of Structural Competition
Competition is a zero sum game, in which the winner is defined by possession of the larger share of the resources at stake. Therefore, when I win, you lose and vice versa. Under conditions of perfect competition, consumers directly influence this distribution of resources by their purchasing behavior. Under conditions of structural competition, firms use marketing strategies to influence consumer behavior and the attendant distribution of resources independently of naturally occurring market forces. To be effective, leaders strive to create structural competition, as they sustain the LMC by

deploying strategies that maximize the quality and number of adherents, the degree of visibility, and access to financial and material resources to support.

Here is a case in point: In an effort to meet his campaign promise of smaller government, Georgia's Governor Sonny Perdue challenged officials of financially strapped hospitals to compete with equally strapped schools for a $30 million line item in the state's budget, thus using conflict as a strategy to reduce the cost of government (Tucker, 2003). Governor Perdue is also a competitive individual: more than once he has run for election and won. One could argue that this competitive approach to cost cutting can also enhance the sustainability of his leadership, by increasing cohesion and collaboration among his supporters. (Note: Two years later, Perdue won the 2006 governor's race in Georgia, in an election that ran counter to a national trend of rejecting Republican leadership.) Such consistency suggests that Governor Perdue experiences few inner or external conflicts about competition as a blend of conflict and collaboration. Indeed, his success reflects an embrace of competition that uncritically privileges conflict as well as collaboration.

On the other hand, lifelong Democrats and political liberals in the state of Georgia are hard pressed to compete with a conflictual approach, given their longstanding philosophical commitment to inclusivity and collaboration. This is the subtext behind the idea of "becoming more like Republicans" mentioned earlier in this essay. Until Georgia's liberal leaders recognize and embrace the *both-and-ness* of conflict and collaboration in competition, they will continue to be at a disadvantage in a winner-take-all environment. Ironically, for these leaders, reframing the traditional liberal view of competition as evil is key to improving the competitive position of collaboration as good.

For-Profit Business Struggles with *Both-And-Ness*

Leaders in business are those who help their companies win conflicts for market domination by promoting collaboration within the LMC known as a firm and by building collaborations with other firms. For example, consider the impenetrable web of relationships that unite commercial airlines and at the same time divide them into competitors. Similarly, nonprofit organizations compete for funding from United Way at the same time as their employees donate to the United Way's annual campaign. These leaders are supported by a multi-billion-dollar-a-year industry in leadership development and coaching (in my day job, I am an infinitesimally small part of that sector). Day rates for experts in the field range from free to tens of thousands of dollars, as established and erstwhile leaders hone their skills and cultivate their talents for leadership.

In the conflict for market domination among leadership developers, the main weapons are catchphrases that capture the attention of adherents, garner easy visibility, and thus secure major resources, e.g., consulting fees. While experience clearly demonstrates the *both-and-ness* of conflict and collaboration in everyday business life, business writers struggle mightily to find the catchphrase to describe these phenomena as a single activity, instead of a perpetual to and fro. What much of what this writing urges business leaders to do is to move away from conflict and focus on the skills of collaboration in order to compete. Here are some examples from the business literature.

IBM Executive Curt Franz (1992) advocated that IBM'ers "take action to reduce competition in our lives and the lives of others [and] educate others about the above" (p. 2). Franz coined the term *commuprove* to designate the activity of cooperatively challenging each other to excel (pp. 23–26). B. J. Nalebuff and A. M. Brandenburger (1997) offered the concept of *co-opetition*, which positions creating and capturing value as two separate activities, analogous to making a pie and working independently to make sure you get the biggest slice of that pie. Dee Hock (1999) coined the term *chaordic* to describe the blend of chaos and order required for success in a changing environment. Taking a broader view, in *The Death of Competition*, J. F. Moore (1996) suggested revamping the whole business lexicon. Arguing that competitive advantage stemmed from "cooperative, coevolving relationships with a network of other contributors to the overall economic scene," he proposed using the term *business ecosystem* instead of the word "industry." Celebrating this co-evolution, Moore suggests that the stability of a large interdependent system creates ample opportunities for new players—"the business equivalents of the mites [which hitchhike on the beaks of hummingbirds to feast on the pollen of the flowers in a tropical rainforest]—to join the ecosystem." As the mites compete for an increased share of margins, leaders learn how to emphasize cooperation to "hold adherents and keep the community rationalizing and improving" (pp. 190–192).

Peter Vaill (1989) used the metaphor of snake-handling to denote acts of blind faith by business managers, be they mites or hummingbirds. This conjures up images of backwoods preachers extending a longstanding folk tradition of taking up serpents. Business leaders, acting on blind faith, wrestle with vipers when they blithely advocate collaboration as a strategy in the conflict for market domination. Like snake-handling religionists, they somehow believe that even if a viper bites, they will not be hurt, that in fact they will be strengthened (Holy Bible: Mark 16:17–18). Vaill challenged the folk traditions of managers by asking them to replace snake-handling with a more solid connection to reality. Building on Vaill's metaphor, by understanding the *both-and-ness* of conflict and collaboration as part of competition, business leaders can begin to make friends with this slithery, shape-changing critter who could kill you in a heartbeat. This in turn might redirect the currently snake-bit efforts to find a catchphrase that describes the phenomenon.

 WHILE EXPERIENCE CLEARLY DEMONSTRATES THE *BOTH-AND-NESS* OF CONFLICT AND COLLABORATION IN EVERYDAY BUSINESS LIFE, BUSINESS WRITERS STRUGGLE MIGHTILY TO FIND THE CATCHPHRASE TO DESCRIBE THESE PHENOMENA AS A SINGLE ACTIVITY, INSTEAD OF A PERPETUAL TO AND FRO.

Seeing Competition (*both-and* of conflict and collaboration) as Messages within the LMC

Nearly two hundred years after Adam Smith first enunciated his economic theory of markets, economist Albert O. Hirschman (1970) observed that increased competition acts as a communication channel by creating an exit option for consumers. Competition in the form of a choice of provider allows consumers to inflict losses on a merchant by taking their business elsewhere. The opposite of exit is loyalty, in which the consumer continues the relationship (Hirschman, 1970, p. 21). Hirschman suggests that this exit may happen silently, without complaint, or may be accompanied by voice, as dissatisfied consumers tell the merchant why they are leaving. On the other hand, loyalty is also a choice, which may be accompanied by silence or by voice in the form of criticism or praise. In Hirschman's model, exit is either silent or accompanied by voice as the consumer raises a critical voice in discussions with the merchant.

Applying this model to leadership deepens our understanding of competition as an embodiment of conflict and collaboration. Conflict occurs when members exit the LMC (e.g., choose another leader), thus inflicting losses on the leader who ignored their feedback and permitted the quality of relationships (e.g., collaboration) with and within the LMC to deteriorate. While exit and vocal loyalty may both be messages that the offering should be improved, the absence of voice says nothing about loyalty. Leaders who assume that no news is good news in a competitive environment may be taking an unnecessary risk for the future of their LMC, as shown in Figure 1 (see page 34).

Figure 2 (see page 35) deepens the communications framework by combining the sender (e.g., member) oriented point of view in Figure 1 with a receiver (e.g., leader) oriented point of view. In this context, deafness on the part of the leader may

Figure 1: Competition as Messages from the Environment

		Exit (Poorer Collaboration for the LMC)		
Voice (Higher Level of Conflict for the LMC)		Members communicate concerns, and if those concerns are not met, they leave the LMC.	Members do not communicate concerns and they leave the LMC.	**Silence** (Lower Level of Conflict for the LMC)
		Members communicate concerns, and if those concerns are not met, they stay with the LMC anyway.	Members have no concerns or fail to communicate concerns and they stay with the LMC.	
		Loyalty (Better Collaboration for the LMC)		

be perceived as conflict, manifest in a refusal to listen to the voices of the LMC and/ or the external environment. If competitive choices are available, such deafness may risk the sustainability of the LMC and its work. In contrast, leaders who attend to the voices of others may be perceived as collaborative, whether or not the leader actually changes position in response to what is heard.

Leader responsiveness is important whether it takes the form of collaboration (a change in position) or conflict (no change in position). When the leader offers a considered rationale that reflects what the leader has heard, there is a sense of collaboration. When the leader fails to respond or responds intransigently to what is heard, this may be perceived as conflict. Such an approach begins to make explicit the complexity of leadership communications and the leader's specific skills in listening for, understanding, and responding to the *both-and-ness* of conflict and collaboration within the LMC.

This matrix begins to illuminate the *both-and-ness* of conflict and collaboration that underlies the role of competition in sustainable leadership. It also provides an initial framework for exploring the multiple dimensions of competition that occur in the reciprocating relationships of political, business and nonprofit, and community leaders. With increased understanding of its role and implications in leadership, competition can be less of a Jungian shadow, the unknown side of a leader's

Figure 2: Interpreting Competition from the Leader Point of View

	Leader Intransigence = Member Exit (Poorer Collaboration for the LMC)		
Member Voice = Leader Hearing (Higher Level of Conflict for the LMC)	Members communicate concerns, and if those concerns are not met, they leave the LMC. Leaders listen to and acknowledge the conflictual voices of members and elect to remain in conflict with alternative points of view.	Members do not communicate concerns and they leave the LMC. Leaders regard such departures as betrayals or conflicts, and as a result fail to benefit from the knowledge embodied by the departure of members.	**Member Silence = Leader Deafness** (Lower Level of Conflict for the LMC)
	Members communicate concerns, and if those concerns are not met, they stay with the LMC anyway. Leaders listen to and acknowledge the conflictual voices of members and, based on this, collaborate by changing position or explaining why they do not.	Members have no concerns or fail to communicate concerns and they stay with the LMC. Leaders privilege collaboration and cohesion over valuable information members bring from diverse points of view.	
	Leader Responsiveness = Member Loyalty (Better Collaboration for the LMC)		

experience. Leaders can better know how to address internal conflicts that currently manifest in sometimes consistent, sometimes confounding public and private behaviors. Finally, leaders themselves can be more skilled in sustaining their leadership by engaging in the competition for adherents, visibility, and resources in the democratic marketplace of ideas.

REFERENCES

Franz, K. (1992). *Cultural heresy: The case against competition.* (Presentation given to IBM audiences). IBM Corporation.

Heilbroner, R., & Thurow, L. (1998). *Economics explained: Everything you need to know about how the economy works and where it's going.* Carmichael, CA: Touchstone Books.

Hirschman, A. O. (1970). *Exit, voice and loyalty.* Cambridge MA: Harvard University Press.

Hock, D. (1999). Keynote address. *International Conference on Servant Leadership.*

Jung, K. (1951). Aion. CW 9, Part II: p.14. Retrieved April 15, 2007, from http://psikoloji.fisek.com.tr/jung/shadow.htm

Merriam-Webster Online Dictionary. Retrieved April 2, 2002, from http://www.merriam-webster.com

Moore, J. F. (1996). *The death of competition: Leadership and strategy in the age of business ecosystems* (1st ed.). New York: HarperCollins.

Nalebuff, B. J., & Brandenburger, A. M. (1997). Co-opetition: Competitive and cooperative business strategies for the digital economy. *Strategy Leadership Resources*, pp. 24–28.

National Public Radio. (2007, April 6). *Morning Edition.*

Northouse, P. G. (2001). *Leadership: Theory and practice* (2nd ed.). Thousand Oaks, CA: Sage Publications.

Putnam, R. (2000). *Bowling alone: The collapse and revival of American community.* New York: Simon & Schuster.

Rechtman, J. (1997). *Field notes: Comments from leaders.* Atlanta, GA: Rechtman Consulting Group.

Smith, A. *An inquiry into the nature and causes of the wealth of nations.* Library of Economics and Liberty. Retrieved April 30, 2007, from http://www.econlib.org/LIBRARY/Smith/smWN1.html

Tucker, C. (2003, November 28). Seems budget can't afford fairness. *Atlanta Journal Constitution,* p. A22.

Vaill, P. (1989). *Managing as a performing art.* San Francisco: Jossey-Bass.

JANET RECHTMAN is an independent consultant in Atlanta, Georgia, who specializes in helping non-profit and community-based leaders embrace the challenges of internal and external collaboration. Janet has her BA from Emory University in Atlanta, a master's from York University in Toronto, and is currently a doctoral candidate in the PhD in Leadership and Change program at Antioch University. She teaches a graduate course in nonprofit marketing at the Andrew Young School of Policy Studies at Georgia State University. She has conducted workshops at a number of national conferences including the Greenleaf Center for Servant Leadership, the International Association of Facilitators, the Community Leadership Association, Southeastern Councils of Foundations, Georgia Gerontology Society, and the International Leadership Association.

The Leader's Role in Cultivating Intuition in the Workplace

By Tom Culham

OUR SOCIETY HAS BENEFITED GREATLY FROM THE WIDESPREAD training of leaders in a foundation of reason and logic in specialties such as business, accounting, law, engineering, medicine, etc. Yet now more than ever it seems we live in a dramatically changing business world with hyper competition, demanding customers, and the rise and fall of whole business sectors, to name a few challenges. Leaders must make decisions with imperfect data in an uncertain world. It is increasingly recognized that the skills acquired in our formal training may not be enough to succeed in the business world. For example, Thomas A. Stewart, editorial director of *Business 2.0*, said, "People who make decisions for a living are coming to realize that in complex or chaotic situations—a battlefield, a trading floor or today's brutally competitive business environment—intuition usually beats rational analysis. And as science looks closer, it is coming to see that intuition is not a gift but a skill. And, like any skill, it's something one can learn" (Stewart, 2002).

"Research shows that decision-makers who qualify as highly intuitive make better decisions in a simulated managerial environment" (Cosier & Aplin, 1982, p. 280). Further, "people who tend to be promoted in organizations typically display more intuitive abilities than do others in the same organizational population" (Fields, 2001, p. 85). Given the limitations of rational decision making and the demonstrated effectiveness of intuition in decision making, the Marine Corps has adopted intuitive approaches in their decision-making processes. Their official doctrine reads, "The intuitive approach is more appropriate for the vast majority of . . . decisions made in the fluid, rapidly changing conditions of war when time and uncertainty are critical factors, and creativity is a desirable trait" (Stewart, 2002). The U.S. Air Force is considering including intuitive alongside rational approaches in their decision-making processes (Davis & Kahan, 2007).

Today's rapidly changing, complex, and global business environment may be similar to the conditions of battle described above, and new approaches are often the source of business success. Fred Smith, CEO of Federal Express, "received a C on a college economics paper in which he outlined his idea for an overnight delivery service. His gut told him it would work anyway. He later explained a C was a very good grade for me" (Stewart, 2002). "Howard Schultz had his eureka moment in Milan, Italy, when he realized that leisurely caffeine-and-conversation would work in the United States, too. Market research might have warned him that Americans would never pay $3 for a cup of coffee. But Schultz didn't need research. He just knew he could turn Starbucks into a bigger business, and he began, literally shaking with excitement" (Stewart, 2002). Clearly intuition is an important skill that helps leaders predict and make better future-oriented decisions.

"Many managers report using intuition in their decision-making in spite of the deeply rooted bias against non-rational methods. However, many remain unwilling to acknowledge their use of intuition, fearing negative responses from colleagues" (Fields, 2001, p. 2). While intuition is an important skill in decision making, it plays second fiddle to rational methods. Einstein observed: "The intuitive mind is a sacred gift and the rational mind is a faithful servant. We have created a society that honors the servant and has forgotten the gift."

Currently, business decisions are informed predominantly by rational thought processes. It is hoped that this paper will help to legitimize intuition and empower leaders to utilize intuition, in conjunction with rational processes, appropriately and openly with confidence in their day-to-day decision making. This will have an impact on our business and social cultures by providing society with better use of what Einstein refers to as the forgotten gift. Ultimately, the sustainability of our planet may be enhanced through better decision making.

What Is Intuition?

Intuition is defined as the power or faculty of attaining direct knowledge or cognition without evident rational thought and inference (Merriam-Webster Online). Definitions provided in organizational engineering methodology include "a way of perceiving which relies on relationships, meanings, and possibilities beyond the reach of the conscious mind and includes behavioural attributes" and "a way of knowing in which we often do not know how we know what we know" (Fields, 2001, p. 7).

Studies conducted by Princeton Engineering Anomalies Research over a twenty-plus-year period indicate that people can send and receive information non-locally (Jahn & Dunne, 1997, 2001). Their research demonstrates that anyone has the ability to influence the output of random number generators at a distance with their thoughts. It has also been scientifically demonstrated that people have remote perception abilities. The former is a process of sending information out while the latter is a process of receiving information from external sources, which might be called a form of intuition. The authors proposed that these findings will have profound implications for science, which we will not elaborate on here.

 INTUITION IS DEFINED AS THE POWER OR FACULTY OF ATTAINING DIRECT KNOWLEDGE OR COGNITION WITHOUT EVIDENT RATIONAL THOUGHT AND INFERENCE.

Psychologists have observed that people with dominance in intuitive thinking bring a particular skill set to their personal relationships and work. They have the ability to bring up new possibilities, supply ingenuity on problems, read signs of coming change, and better prepare for the future (Myers & Myers, 1995). Persons with intuitive ability have the necessary skills to manage change, manage complexity, manage conflict, and contribute to creative processes (Parikh, Neubauer, & Lank, 1996). These are all desirable qualities in today's complex and rapidly changing business environment. This gives rise to several questions for leaders. How does one recognize those naturally endowed with intuitive skills? (After all, there are no schools or qualifications that formally train or recognize intuitive skills.) How does one deploy people who have intuitive skills? How does one develop intuitive skills personally and within the organization?

Recognizing Intuitive Skills
Practically, recognition of people with intuitive skills can be achieved in two ways—through application of the Myers-Brigg personality test and through observation of people in the workplace. For those observing others, they will be assisted by familiarizing themselves with the Myers-Briggs personality classification system. In particular, they will benefit from understanding the differences between sensing and intuitive types. A description of how the different types contribute, communicate, and obtain information differently is provided in the table on the following page. The Myers-Briggs test has been shown to correlate with intuitive skills in laboratory tests (Radin, 2006).

Engaging Those with Intuitive Skills
After recognizing those with intuitive skills, the leader faces two related challenges in successfully engaging these employees. First, there is a bias against the use of intuition

Sensing and Intuitive Types Contrasted

Sensing Types	Intuitive Types
Contribute by Bringing up pertinent facts; Applying experience to problems; Reading the fine print in a contract; Noticing what needs attention now; Having patience; Keeping track of essential details; and Facing difficulties with realism	**Contribute by** Bringing up new possibilities; Supplying ingenuity on problems; Reading the signs of coming change; Seeing how to prepare for the future; Having enthusiasm; Watching for new essentials; and Tackling difficulties with zest
Communicate with A nonjudgmental presentation of facts concerning the past or present	**Communicate with** A future-oriented, and often exaggerated, scattered flow of thoughts
Obtain Information Externally through their five senses	**Obtain Information** Internally through intuitions that come up from their unconscious that can be hunches, gut feelings, and original ideas

Sources: Myers & Myers, 1995; Thompson, 1997

in the workplace (Fields, 2001). Second, almost three-quarters of the population of the U.S. has a preference for sensing approaches, which puts intuitive types in the minority (Keirsey & Bates, 1984). Given the bias against intuitive decision making, organizations therefore are likely to favour the communication style and approach of individuals consistent with a rational style of decision making.

The predominance of sensing types in the general population may be represented in the workplace, and this has implications as well. Psychologists have observed that more sympathy, approval, and comfort can be expected for types that are alike while types that reflect different strengths and values may not seem as desirable (Myers & Myers, 1995). It is not surprising that people who think alike are able to communicate more readily, maybe even more efficiently, but are they able to be as productive for the business?

The leader, therefore, needs to recognize that those with intuitive abilities communicate and contribute in ways that are different than are expected in a culture where intuitive decision making is discouraged and sensing types are the majority. Also, he or she needs to develop interpersonal leadership competencies personally and in others so that the organization is better able to obtain and benefit from the contributions of a diversity of employees.

The difficulty in managing communications and obtaining contributions from both sensing and intuitive types is evident in brainstorming sessions. One of the primary brainstorming rules is no judging of others' ideas during the idea-generation phase. Those types who prefer to judge must switch to a more open or perceptive language mode during the entire session. This can be a difficult task. The intuitive person is likely to be comfortable with the open, random, and sometimes wacky ideas produced in a brainstorming session while the sensing type who prefers to deal with facts, a focused agenda, and purposeful action will find it a challenge to hold back judgment and criticism for what may seem to them a frivolous process (Thompson, 1997).

 THE INTUITIVE PERSON IS LIKELY TO BE COMFORTABLE WITH THE OPEN, RANDOM, AND SOMETIMES WACKY IDEAS PRODUCED IN A BRAINSTORMING SESSION . . .

An example of a well-developed activity for managing differences is the cross-functional team, which is used to encourage contribution from all participants in a group of people with different levels of authority, perspectives, and skill sets. This is usually supported through the establishment and management of team norms by a facilitator trained in eliciting input from a cross-section of team members. An example of team norms for the operation of a cross-functional team might include the following: express views and challenge each other's thinking; listen and seek clarification and understanding; treat each other with respect; deal with the issue, not the person; the entire team must sign off on major decisions; ask for time before committing if reflection is needed; if the team convenes with a member absent, brief the member immediately upon return and revisit pending decisions; and use each other's strengths —trust each other. These norms demonstrate an objective of engendering trust, which provides participants with confidence in their ideas and means processing information will be respected. Coupled with an awareness of the contribution of the intuitive style, the application and use of interpersonal leadership competencies will assist in valuing, integrating, and fully engaging those with an intuitive approach.

Developing Intuitive Skills

Although the process of developing intuitive skills is not well understood, Princeton Engineering Anomalies Research (PEAR) has discovered some practical recommendations for enhancing intuitive skills which are useful for our purposes (Jahn & Dunne, 2001). The researchers concluded a person can improve their intuitive skills if the individual:

    1. is amenable to surrendering a precise focus;

    2. has the intention of sending or receiving information;

    3. surrenders conscious control of or investment in the process, that is, does not try too hard; and

    4. allows the mind to enter a fuzzy state or allows the subconscious mind to rise.

While the list above is important in the intuitive process, PEAR identified the subconscious mind as critical in the intuitive process of sending or receiving information (Jahn & Dunne, 2001). The purpose of starting with a conscious intention, not trying too hard for results, and letting the mind enter a fuzzy state is to allow the intuitive information in the subconscious mind to come to the surface and enter conscious awareness. Stated another way, to be effective from the perspective of receiving information intuitively, one must consciously decide to be open to intuitive information, to not try too hard to receive information, and to let go of the conscious mind (enter a fuzzy state of mind) to give the subconscious the opportunity to access and reveal the information. Given this, it is understandable that snap decisions, sleeping on a decision, or stepping away from thinking about a decision enhances decision-making quality. These strategies set the conscious mind aside and allow the subconscious to function. The subconscious is defined as "existing in the mind but not immediately available to consciousness" (Merriam-Webster Online). For a discussion of the meaning of *subconscious* refer to Jahn and Dunne (2001, p. 308).

It has been established that the subconscious and the body are connected (Pert, 1999). Intuitive skills may be developed through practicing contemplative disciplines such as yoga, tai chi, qigong, and meditation. They all attend to the management and integration of three elements—breath, posture, and mind. Instead of focusing only on conscious thought, which is common in logical thought processes, attention in these disciplines is distributed amongst the three. Qigong, for example, is a holistic system of self-healing exercise and meditation, an ancient evolving practice that includes healing posture, movement, self-massage, breathing techniques, and meditation (Cohen, 1999). Therefore, these disciplines with their balanced approach help to integrate body and mind, subconscious and conscious. The outcome is the practitioner has easier access to information contained in or entering the subconscious mind, thereby enhancing intuitive skills. One could argue that these contemplative disciplines are practices that improve intuitive abilities (Culham, 2003).

Medical anthropologists observing the training of traditional Chinese medical qigong noticed that the student doctors acquired intuitive knowledge. It was observed that "the style of knowledge the student acquires in the practice of medical qigong is characterized by the automatism of bodily movements, on the one hand, and the unpredictability of spiritual experiences on the other. This style of knowing included the ability to enter and leave qigong states of knowledge. In addition the acquisition of knowledge was marked by uncertainty. The knowledge was not always accessible; it presented itself in different ways and it sometimes bore the danger of overwhelming the person who had achieved access to it" (Hsu, 1999, p. 49). A qigong state of knowledge obtains where highly trained practitioners are able to access knowledge intuitively or directly without the use of the senses.

The Leader's Role in Cultivating Intuition

What is a leader to do with this knowledge? In simple terms, when making big decisions which entail assimilating complex or ambiguous information it makes sense to sleep on it or step away from the decision and do something else for a while. This gives the subconscious mind an opportunity to process data. Just as companies today encourage employees to stay physically fit through fitness programs and annual health checkups, companies may wish to provide incentives for employees to provide intuitive fitness through meditation, yoga, tai chi, or qigong. Leaders may try these practices, preferably under the guidance of a qualified instructor, and they must have the patience to be open to alternative forms of information and keen observation skills. They have spent half a lifetime learning logical processes in our education system. Learning to be intuitive is an organic process that takes time and practice.

 JUST AS COMPANIES TODAY ENCOURAGE EMPLOYEES TO STAY PHYSICALLY FIT THROUGH FITNESS PROGRAMS AND ANNUAL HEALTH CHECKUPS, COMPANIES MAY WISH TO PROVIDE INCENTIVES FOR EMPLOYEES TO PROVIDE INTUITIVE FITNESS THROUGH MEDITATION, YOGA, TAI CHI, OR QIGONG.

Organizations would likely benefit if leaders and individuals familiarized themselves with the nature of how intuitive information presents itself; otherwise it may be dismissed or lost. It does not appear as a number on a spreadsheet at the end of a long formula. Rather, intuitive information can come at any time and place in the form of visions, feelings, dreams, random thoughts, etc. It is not predictable, can be paradoxical, may not be limited by time or space, is not sequential, and usually is holistic. One can see that for those trained in logical thought processes, intuitive ideas can easily be dismissed.

A Personal Experience

To illustrate my interest in cultivating intuition, I relate here a brief experience from early in my career. At the time, I was a researcher analyzing reams of satellite imagery data that in those days came in the form of numbers representing the intensity of light reflected from the earth. I had the job of developing analytical tools for interpreting the data. I printed out the data and simply looked over sheet after sheet of raw numbers. After completing this cursory review I had the feeling a specific analytical tool would be useful for our purposes. When I met with my supervisor and told him my idea he asked me, "How do you know this?" I said, "I looked over the data. It's just a feeling, but I don't know the reason." He looked at me as if there was something wrong with me. Later, after much analysis, it turned out the idea I had originally proposed was very useful.

Developing intuitive skills and utilizing them is a journey for which a proven map has not been developed. My intent in this article is to provide some indication of the reasons why it is important to recognize, manage, and develop intuitive skills. I believe this is a new practice with much room for the introduction of new knowledge and improvement.

I wish to close by repeating Einstein's observation, "The intuitive mind is a sacred gift and the rational mind is a faithful servant. We have created a society that honors the servant and has forgotten the gift." I believe that working toward the goal of putting intuition on an equal footing with rational decision making will be a great benefit to business and society.

REFERENCES

Cohen, K. (1999). *The way of qigong, The art and science of Chinese energy healing* (1st paperback ed.). New York: Ballantine.

Cosier, R. A., & Aplin, J. C. (1982). Intuition and decision making: Some empirical evidence. *Psychological Reports, 51,* 275–281.

Culham, T. (2003). *An exploration of a mind body discipline qigong and a possible contribution to science.* Seminar for The David See Chai Lam Center for International Communication, Simon Fraser University.

Davis, P. K., & Kahan, J. P. (2007). *Theory and methods for supporting high level military decision making.* Report prepared for the United States Air Force, The Rand Corporation Technical Report Series.

Fields, A. F. (2001). *A study of intuition in decision-making using organizational engineering methodology.* A dissertation submitted to Wayne Huizenga Graduate School of Business and Entrepreneurship of Nova Southeastern University, in partial fulfillment of the requirements for the degree of Doctor of Business Administration.

Hsu, E. (1999). *The transmission of Chinese medicine.* The Edinburgh Building, Cambridge, UK: Cambridge University Press.

Jahn, R., & Dunne, B. (1997). *Science of the subjective.* Princeton Engineering Anomalies Research Laboratory, School of Engineering and Applied Science, Princeton University. Reprint of an essay originally published in the *Journal of Scientific Exploration, 11*(2) 201–224.

Jahn, R., & Dunne, B. (2001). A modular model of mind/matter manifestations. *Journal of Scientific Exploration, 15*(3), 299–329.

Kiersey, D., & Bates, M. (1984). *Please understand me: Character and temperament types* (3rd ed.). Del Mar, CA: Prometheus.

Merriam-Webster Online, http://www.m-w.com/dictionary/intuition and http://www.m-w.com/dictionary/subconscious

Myers, I., & Myers, P. (1995). *Gifts differing: Understanding personality type.* Palo Alto, CA: Davies-Black Publishing.

Parikh, J., Neubauer, F., & Lank, A. (1996). *Intuition: The new frontier of management.* Oxford, UK: Blackwell Publishers Ltd.

Pert, C. (1999). *Molecules of emotion: The science behind mind-body medicine.* New York: Scribner.

Radin, D. (2006). *Entangled minds: Extrasensory experiences in a quantum reality.* New York: Paraview Pocket Books.

Stewart, T. A. (2002). *How to think with your gut.* Retrieved from http://money.cnn.com/magazines/business2/business2_archive/2002/11/01/331634/index.htm

Thompson, H. (1997). *Type languages, dialects, styles and the extraverted function: Is there a relationship?* Retrieved from http://www.hpsys.com/Articles/Type_Languages_Dialects_Styles_Extraverted.htm

TOM CULHAM is a professional engineer with twenty-seven years in business, holding leadership positions predominantly in the resource sector based in Vancouver, Canada. He recently entered the field of higher education as an adjunct faculty member with City University, and is currently working on his PhD in educational philosophy at Simon Fraser University. Tom is Principal of the consulting firm Culham Business Solutions Ltd.

Ethical Perspectives of Transformational Leadership

Are Ethical Leaders Transformational or Are Transformational Leaders Ethical?

By Kathie L. Pelletier

THE TOPICS OF TRANSFORMATIONAL LEADERSHIP (BASS, 1985; BURNS, 1978) and organizational ethics (Bartels, 1967; Hunt & Vitell, 1986) have been researched for decades as relatively independent concepts, with any overlap being an afterthought rather than a function of planned research hypotheses. As an increasing number of organizations are experiencing the consequences of ethical misconduct, many are turning to organizational psychologists and business consultants for appropriate interventions. Consequently, a stream of ethics research is now making its way into leadership and business ethics journals. The research that is being conducted focuses primarily on how business leaders can influence ethical behavior in organizations (Bass & Steidlmeier, 1999; Kanungo, 2001; Mendonca, 2001). Specifically, the research appears to be concentrated on the positive aspects of transformational leadership and how the four characteristics of transformational leadership pertain to organizational ethics.

How are organizational ethics relevant to the topic of leadership? The familiar adage "When in Rome, do as the Romans do" has been passed down through the centuries as a practical guide to general behavior which would include business relationships (Minkes, Small, & Chatterjee, 1999). However, when "doing as the Romans do" involves behaving in an unethical manner, an intervention in the form of strong ethical leadership would be prudent to deploy. In some organizations, top leaders may not be stellar examples of moral behavior but may be able to influence followers based on their charismatic ability. In addition, the influence might not be leading followers in the right direction.

Several recent examples in the organizational world illustrate the detrimental impact of unethical decision making. Consider the unethical organizational practices that included fraudulent billing for Medicaid services, the moral failings of the United States' tobacco industry by attempting to lure children to pick up a vice that could eventually kill them (Schwarz, 2001), Enron's scheme to illegally manipulate prices in California's energy market, and the subsequent shredding of evidential documents by the consulting firm of Arthur Andersen (Cohan, 2002) to avoid being implicated in the scandal. These factors have resulted in a crisis of trust and confidence in the institutions in American government and corporate America that have traditionally been a source of leadership. Further, cherished institutions such as churches have not been immune to the consequences of improprieties. There is an even stronger case for crises brought about by a lack of trust if one considers the surfacing of numerous allegations of sexual misconduct of priests in the Catholic Church. Now, more than ever, organizations and their members need guidance in creating an ethical organizational culture to stimulate morally responsible behavior.

Establishing an ethical organizational culture is not without its challenges. In any organization there is likely to be a climate of opinion and behavior that is reflected both in member perceptions of expectations and in their expectations as to what they are likely to receive in response to "good" performance. It is widely accepted that part of the function of the organization's leadership is to articulate those expectations and to establish the norms that govern the behavior of employees. For these reasons, integrity in leadership (i.e., ethical leadership) is becoming an increasing concern within business and organizations, and the field of organizational behavior has been examining the influential characteristics of transformational leadership to determine the optimal leadership intervention.

The ability of leaders to have profound influences on follower attitudes and behavior is prevalent in transformational leadership style; therefore, it makes sense that this style of leadership would be optimal for an organization that is seeking to build or reestablish an ethical culture. Guiding this review are several key questions: Are leaders considered ethical because they are transformational, or are leaders considered to be transformational because they are ethical? Further, to what extent does the ethical component of transformational leadership actually influence moral reasoning? The author, in agreement with Bass and Steidlmeier (1999), contends that leaders must be ethical to be considered authentically transformational. The purpose of this paper is to describe characteristics of transformational leadership and dimensions of ethical leadership, present theoretical viewpoints on both topics, present and evaluate empirical findings related to the characteristics that operationalize transformational leadership in relation to ethical leadership, and discuss implications of transformational leadership and ethics for research and practice. For the purpose of this literature review, the term "ethical" means that which is morally good or that which is considered morally right, as opposed to that which is legally or procedurally right (Kanungo, 2001).

 NOW, MORE THAN EVER, ORGANIZATIONS AND THEIR MEMBERS NEED GUIDANCE IN CREATING AN ETHICAL ORGANIZATIONAL CULTURE TO STIMULATE MORALLY RESPONSIBLE BEHAVIOR. **""**

Transformational Leadership Theory

Transformational leadership literature (Bass & Steidlmeier, 1999; Burns, 1978) suggests authentic transformational leadership must be based on some moral foundation. The foundation is built on the life experiences, education, and interactions with social environment. Burns (1978, p. 403) postulates that anyone can be a transformational leader. Transformational leadership involves not only the moral elevation of individual followers, but also collective efforts to accomplish social reforms. Ethical leaders, like transformational leaders, appeal to ideals and moral values such as justice, equality, and humanitarianism. In the process, both the leaders and followers are changed.

According to Bass (1985), transformational leadership can be operationalized into four dimensions: charisma (i.e., idealized influence), inspirational motivation, intellectual stimulation, and individualized consideration. Followers describe their charismatic leaders as those who elicit enthusiasm, command respect from everyone, and have a special gift of seeing what is important. Followers describe leader charisma as the ability of leaders to influence ideals by transmitting a sense of mission to followers through visioning and persuasive appeals (Conger & Kanungo, 1998). Inspirational motivation involves the arousal and heightening of initiative among followers; intellectual stimulation triggers the awareness of problems and ways of solving them, stirs the imagination, and generates thoughts and insights. Finally, individualized consideration involves giving personal attention to followers by treating each person individually and helping each individual get what he or she wants (Bass, 1985). The underlying factor to the four dimensions is the absence of ego and self-serving interest on the part of the leader.

Transformational leadership holds great promise for guiding an organization down an ethical path because it can cause fundamental change. The goals of leader and followers may have initially been different, but they eventually coalesce into a common goal. Transformational leadership is also known as elevating, mobilizing, inspiring, uplifting, and exalting (Banerji & Krishnan, 2000). This leadership style becomes moral by raising the level of human conduct and ethical aspiration of both the leader and the led. Transformational leadership is also concerned with end-values such as liberty, equality, and justice, and these three concepts are widely encompassed in ethical principles.

Theoretical Dimensions of Ethical Leadership

To judge a leader's behavior to be ethical or unethical, regardless of the type of influence mode (i.e., leadership style), the following should be considered: the motive of the leader, which is the primary source of one's behavior; the behavior that is exhibited and how it is exhibited; and the social context in which the behavior takes place (Kanungo, 2001). Taking these three factors into account, the leader, to be ethical, must engage in virtuous acts or behaviors that benefit others (i.e., be pure in motive) and must refrain from unethical acts or behaviors that harm others, regardless of the situation. These acts must stem from the leader's altruistic rather than egotistic motives or intentions. Further, to behave in an ethical manner, the leader must consider the demands of the social context or situation he or she faces and the moral consequences of his or her actions in that situation.

Brown and Treviño (2006), and Pelletier and Bligh (2006), defined ethical leadership as the ability of leaders to influence employees to make ethical decisions through role modeling, coaching, the ability to embed a culture of trust, and by acknowledging and supporting ethical decision making. Taking these researchers' viewpoints into account, and coupling them with Kanungo's (2001) assertions, one can begin to understand the association between qualities of ethical leadership and the characteristics of transformational leadership.

Linkage between Transformational Leadership and
Ethical Leadership Theories

The similarity between transformational leadership characteristics and dimensions of ethical leadership can be seen first in idealized influence, or charisma. According to Bass (1985), idealized influence arouses strong follower emotions and identification with the leader. The influence process is successful because the leader appeals to followers' values and those values are salient for both the leader and the followers.

The second characteristic of transformational leadership is inspirational motivation. Conger (1999) suggested that transformational leaders lead by example through role modeling. While role modeling, leaders tend to rely on charismatic leadership skills and seek to "inspirationally motivate" followers to act ethically by exhibiting the behaviors they would like their subordinates to model. To the extent leaders "walk the talk" in terms of ethical behavior, followers are likely to follow suit (McDonald & Nijhof, 1999). Transformational leaders also strive to enhance meaningfulness of goals and behaviors. One way they do this is by ensuring organizations include a statement regarding ethical expectations within a formal ethics code or mission statement. Although the passage of the Sarbanes-Oxley Act has been instrumental in facilitating the development of ethical codes of conduct in organizations that are publicly traded (Paine, Deshpandé, Margolis, & Bettcher, 2005), transformational leaders are noted for their ability to articulate ethical expectations in meaningful ways, beyond statements on paper. On a deeper level, transformational leaders are able to articulate a vision of an ethical organization while encouraging behavior toward ethical objectives.

Turning to individualized consideration, the third transformational leadership characteristic, an "individually considerate" leader gives personal attention to his or her followers, treating them as unique persons while encouraging self-development. When faced with an ethical dilemma, the overlap between the individualized consideration characteristic and ethical leadership is based on the leader considering the follower and making decisions that ensure followers are not harmed. It is reasonable to expect that transformational leaders are more likely to include fellow workers within their scope of justice, justice being an ethical outcome of ethical deliberation (Margaret, 2003). Simply stated, scope of justice is the extent to which a leader extends a concern (i.e., concern for equity and fairness) to another, or encourages a subordinate to extend a justice concern to him or her, as well (Singer & Singer, 1997). Moreover, employee self-development is promoted through the candid exchange of moral dialogue between leader and follower and through the development of our interpersonal relationships.

> **ON A DEEPER LEVEL, TRANSFORMATIONAL LEADERS ARE ABLE TO ARTICULATE A VISION OF AN ETHICAL ORGANIZATION WHILE ENCOURAGING BEHAVIOR TOWARD ETHICAL OBJECTIVES.**

Transformational leaders also intellectually stimulate subordinates through arousal of awareness of problems and ways of solving them (Bass, 1985). Leaders who excel at this dimension are able to stir the imagination of followers. This arousal may manifest itself in followers through the generation of new ideas, ethical solutions, or added insight. Similarly, ethical leadership shares themes with intellectual stimulation in that ethical leaders are able to influence employees to make decisions by involving them in ethical discussion and by actively supporting ethical decision making (Pelletier & Bligh, 2006). According to Kanungo (2001), to be ethical, leaders must refrain from unethical acts or behaviors that might harm others. In doing so, ethical leaders role model and intellectually stimulate subordinates in the same manner as transformational leaders.

Further links between ethical and transformational leadership can be found when leaders with integrity encourage open and honest communication, particularly in discussions involving decision making (Parry & Proctor-Thomson, 2002). Leaders with integrity value an individual's viewpoint and the feedback that results from the sharing of opinion. This leadership value is consistent with transformational leadership. Further, the importance of clear vision and the establishment of trust are prime factors contributing to personal and organizational integrity.

After more than three decades of leadership research, scholars are revisiting virtue leadership, a form of leadership that shares commonalities with transformational leadership (Margaret, 2003; Schwartz, 1985; Treddenick, 1969). Central to this leadership literature is the emphasis on Aristotelian virtues or the idea that a harmonious balance of virtues leads to a "good" life (Margaret, 2003). The moral virtues associated with Aristotelian ethics include justice, courage, temperance, honor, congeniality, and truthfulness. If a leader possesses these virtues, then he or she is entitled to the claim of being moral or ethical (Singer & Singer, 1997). Moberg (1999) argues that conscientiousness and agreeableness, two of the "Big Five" personality characteristics suggested by Goldberg (1990), are the most essential virtues of ethical leaders. Conscientious leaders tend to be competent, have orderly work habits, are principled, diligent, and self-disciplined. Agreeable leaders are people who are consistently candid, disposed to trust others, are compliant and sympathetic. In other personnel selection literature, these two dimensions have been identified as key components of the construct "integrity" (Margaret, 2003).

In reviewing dimensions of virtue leadership, one can see the link between virtue leadership and ethical leadership. Ethical leaders are compliant with organizational ethical expectations and hold subordinates accountable for compliance, as well. Moreover, ethical leaders, like transformational leaders, are candid when communicating with followers and exhibit, as well as elicit, trust.

Based on the aforementioned characteristics of ethical and transformational leadership, there is certainly evidence to support the assertion that there is an overlap between these two forms of leadership. As described earlier, transformational leaders demonstrate consideration of their staff on an individual basis, motivate and inspire, provide intellectual challenges, and are considered to promote vision. Further, leaders who are transformational are perceived by their followers to demonstrate self-confidence, exert influence over others, and develop a sense of affiliation. It is apparent that the transformational style of leadership reflects many of the essential components of the traits "conscientiousness" and "agreeableness" as described by Moberg (1999). Conscientious leaders are principled and self-disciplined. Transformational leaders are principled in that they tend to be more concerned with end-values such as liberty, justice, and equality than with means-values (Banerji & Krishnan, 2000). Agreeable leaders are consistently candid and are disposed to trust others. This personality dimension is evident to the extent transformational leaders engage in individualized consideration behaviors.

Theoretically speaking, the overlap between ethical leadership and transformational leadership seems clear; however, when put to the empirical test will there be a relationship between the two? Further, if there is a relationship, will researchers and practitioners know the answer to the proverbial question, "Which came first . . . ?"

 ALTHOUGH THE CORRELATIONAL APPROACH LIMITS ONE'S ABILITY TO IDENTIFY A CAUSAL LINK BETWEEN THE VARIABLES OF INTEREST, IT DOES LEND SOME INSIGHT AS TO HOW TRANSFORMATIONAL LEADERSHIP AND ETHICAL LEADERSHIP ARE RELATED.

Empirical Research: The Chicken or the Egg?

Over the past five years, empirical correlational studies have focused on the similarities between ethical leadership and characteristics of transformational leadership. Although the correlational approach limits one's ability to identify a causal link between the variables of interest, it does lend some insight as to how transformational leadership and ethical leadership are related. There appear to be two questions that are vying for the top seed in leadership and ethics journals: Are leaders ethical because they are transformational? or, Are leaders transformational because they are ethical? Although the definition of transformational leadership assumes leadership is altruistic, moral, and operating for the common good, the "dark side" of charisma surfaces when a leader's vision is focused on egoistic, self-serving, or immoral outcomes. Further, when leaders stimulate followers to follow a grand illusion masquerading as a noble vision, followers may allow themselves to be guided down a dangerous road (Lipman-Blumen, 2005). These phenomena fuel one side of the debate that contends leaders who are transformational may not necessarily be ethical (i.e., they are pseudo-transformational). Leaders who exhibit this "dark side" are likely to lead followers into negative, unethical, and immoral directions (Parry & Proctor-Thomson, 2002).

The debate prompted Parry and Proctor-Thomson (2002) to engage in research to determine if there is an empirical link between integrity and transformational leadership. These researchers posited that the perceived integrity of leaders would be positively correlated with transformational leadership. In addition, they also examined the relationship between perceptions of idealized influence/charisma and perceived leader integrity.

In Parry and Proctor-Thomson's research (2002), a sample of 1,354 managers from both public- and private-sector organizations in New Zealand completed the Multifactor Leadership Questionnaire (MLQ) (Bass & Avolio, 1995) and the Perceived Leader Integrity Scale (PLIS) (Bartholomew & Gustafson, 1998). The PLIS quantifies subordinate perceptions of the integrity of a leader's style of behavior. The scale is comprised of a set of specific unethical leader behaviors of which it is expected that any subordinate in any situation would have knowledge. The MLQ measures both transformational and transactional leadership, including the differentiation of the separate dimensions of both styles.

Parry and Proctor-Thomson (2002) found a significant positive correlation between perceived leader integrity and transformational leadership behaviors. Leaders who were perceived to be high in integrity were perceived to be high in transformational leadership characteristics. Second, they posited that idealized influence (i.e., charisma) would correlate positively with perceived integrity. These researchers obtained a significant and positive correlation between idealized influence and perceptions of leader integrity. These findings provide support for the side of the debate that posits transformational leadership is ethical in nature; however, given their study was correlational, the direction of the relationship remains largely untested.

A body of research that was conducted in Europe and Canada revealed the benefits of transformational leadership on organizational ethical functioning. Turner, Barling, Epitropaki, Butcher, and Milner (2002) argued that transformational leadership should be related to high levels of moral development. These researchers hypothesized that leaders with higher moral reasoning would be perceived by their followers as more transformational than transactional. Specifically, Turner et al. (2002) posited that leaders with more complex moral reasoning would be able to draw on more sophisticated conceptualizations of interpersonal situations and would be more likely to think about problems from multiple perspectives. Leaders with more complex moral reasoning would also be more likely to value goals that transcend immediate self-interest and to foresee the benefits of actions that would serve the collective good. Conversely, these researchers predicted that leaders who see interactions with subordinates as having primarily instrumental ends (transactional leadership) would be less likely to exhibit such transformational behaviors. Simply stated, leaders with higher moral reasoning would be perceived by their subordinates as more transformational.

Turner et al. (2002) tested the hypothesized relationship in three organizational samples drawn from two countries (a Canadian university, a United Kingdom telecommunications company, and a hospital in the United Kingdom). Managers from the three organizations distributed questionnaires to subordinates with whom they had frequent interaction and were asked to complete a separate questionnaire themselves. The managers completed the Defining Issues Test (Rest, 1979) that measures moral reasoning. Subordinate questionnaires contained items from the MLQ that included the five scales used to measure the four dimensions of transformational leadership.

Support was found for Turner et al.'s (2002) hypotheses, lending empirical evidence for theorists who have argued that higher moral development is related to greater use of transformational behaviors. The results of this study lend credence to the debate that to be transformational, leaders must be perceived as possessing high moral reasoning.

In contrast to the two studies mentioned above, there is some support for the notion that leaders are more ethical because they are transformational in terms of follower perceptions. Banerji and Krishnan (2000) looked at the four factors of transformational leadership and the leader's preference for unethical behavior. Specifically, these researchers assumed that different aspects of transformational leadership would be related to differences in evaluations of ethical dilemmas. Five ethical scenarios were presented to a sample of one hundred manager-subordinate pairs from four multinational organizations in India. The video vignettes contained five ethical dilemmas dealing with bribery, endangering the environment, lying, personal gain, and favoritism. Both leader/follower pairs viewed the videos independently and then completed a questionnaire that asked what they would do if faced with that situation. Following this exercise, the subordinates completed the MLQ.

The results of this study showed a negative correlation between inspirational leadership and a leader's preference for bribery and preference for favoritism. Leaders who were perceived to have low preferences for bribery and favoritism were seen as being more inspirationally motivating. Further, a significant negative correlation was found between the intention to bribe and intellectual stimulation. Banerji and Krishnan (2000) explained that leaders who intellectually stimulated followers were likely to lead followers to develop innovative solutions for avoiding occasions of bribery.

Three of the unethical behaviors—endangering the environment, lying, and personal gain—were not related to any of the transformational leadership characteristics. A person could be seen as being highly transformational despite that person preferring any of those three unethical practices. Surprisingly, charisma and individualized consideration were not related to preference for any of the five unethical behaviors. The results of Banerji and Krishnan's (2000) study are puzzling because they fail to support the commonly held assumption that transformational leaders are necessarily ethical.

Where other studies incorporated written scenarios dealing with ethical dilemmas (Parry & Proctor-Thomson, 2002), Banerji and Krishnan's (2000) study used vignettes where both leaders and subordinates indicated the behavior they would display in such a situation. In addition, the menu of ethical dilemmas was varied to enable the subordinate to respond to a diverse array of ethical situations. The use of video vignettes was a faithful representation of ethical dilemmas common in business settings.

Why these results run counter to common wisdom probably lies in knowledge of a broader culture. What is considered prohibited, unethical behavior in the United States might be considered ethically permitted or legally sanctioned in other organizational cultures. The converse is also likely; what is considered unethical in another country might be considered appropriate in the United States. For example, "greasing palms" or offering bribes might be questioned in one culture but may be considered the cost of doing business in another.

Research Gaps: Weaknesses in the Area

Although substantial research has been forthcoming on the topic of transformational leadership and business ethics, there have been weaknesses in the area of transformational leadership study. For example, there has been little research that examines the link between pseudo-transformational leadership, the dark side of charisma, and ethical behavior. According to Aronson (2001), the transformational leadership characteristic of charisma falls along a continuum. The high end of the continuum describes this component in terms of a leader having the ability to influence subordinates through moral and egalitarian behaviors. The transformational leadership charismatic component (idealized influence), at the low end of the continuum, characterizes the leader as being self-aggrandizing, nonegalitarian, and exploitative. Lipman-Blumen (2005) further elaborates on the intensity level of toxic leader behavior that can be considered pseudo-transformational. Behaviors of toxic leaders who may be ethical, but nonetheless are toxic, include incompetence, arrogance, and carelessness. With the overarching motive for ethical leadership being the leader's altruistic intent as opposed to egoistic intent, evaluating follower perceptions of transformational leaders who fall on the low end of this continuum is imperative.

The second gap in the research on ethics and transformational leadership pertains to external validity. The vast majority of the studies conducted focus on follower *perceptions* of leader morality, ethical decision making, or behavior, but does not examine if the leaders' influence actually changes or affects subordinate behavior. This limitation is evident when researchers conclude that ethical leaders are effective based on perception, rather than on actual changes in follower behavior. It is not surprising that this gap exists; one can imagine the difficulty in measuring follower behavior—pre and post leadership intervention—on actions that, if unethical, are usually covert.

Another weakness in the area of ethical measurement concerns a lack of external validity that is prevalent in the types of ethical dilemmas that are currently being used to measure ethical decision making. Researchers have tended to rely on standardized, general scenarios that may not be relevant to a particular organization or sample simply because there is a lack of appropriate measures available. In the studies that were evaluated for the purpose of this paper, it was noted that there were reliable scales that measured the characteristics of transformational leadership, as well as an individual's moral judgment, but no scale that served as a direct measure of the ethical components of transformational leadership.

Future Research Opportunities

The possibilities for future research are considerable. Research should focus on evaluating the effects of the "dark side" of charisma, or pseudo-transformational leadership on followers, developing a more comprehensive set of ethical behavior/ decision-making measures, improving the reliability of ethical measurements, improving external validity of studies through the incorporation of job-relevant ethical dilemmas, and establishing the existence of subordinate behavior change as a result of ethical leadership, rather than changes in follower perceptions of leaders.

Finally, at the dependent variable end of the spectrum is the need to measure actual organizational performance against integrity. The majority of research that has been conducted has focused on perceived organizational or leader effectiveness. If transformational and ethical leadership are considered superlative in terms of influencing followers to achieve a higher level of ethical decision making and moral behavior, practitioners should begin to embark on research that measures actual outcomes, rather than perceived outcomes. Admittedly, this task is a difficult one.

Implications for Practice

Research on organizational leadership and ethics lends itself to limitations based on the very nature of the topics. Both themes involve intrinsic as well as extrinsic qualities, values, attitudes and, finally, behaviors. For decades, researchers have studied leadership from a trait, personality, and behavior perspective, and the field still does not have conclusive findings about how "good" leadership evolves. The debate about whether leadership skills are innate or acquired is still open.

With regard to ethics, researchers acknowledge that ethical values are shaped through childhood experiences. Children learn what is right and wrong from parents, friends, their schools, and/or religious institutions. As these children mature and enter the workforce, one thing is for sure: they will become leaders and followers, and they will all possess values and beliefs about what they consider to be right or wrong. The onus on organizations is to communicate ethical expectations. The onus on leaders is to make ethical choices and create an ethical work environment via the characteristics that define transformational leadership.

The implications for leaders' roles in improving organizational ethics are plentiful. To illustrate, brief examples of foundational recommendations for enhancing ethical behavior in business settings are included here. One implication is for organizations to assess their ethical climates and audit them for the presence of integrity. Paradoxically, identifying ethical climate is rooted in perceptions, which may be unrelated to actual behavior and objective outcomes such as fraud, bribes, and kickbacks, to name a few. A second implication for practice includes recruiting and selecting new employees based on a measure of ethical values or beliefs and evaluating to determine if there is alignment between organizational beliefs and personal beliefs of the prospective employee. The same can be said when organizations seek to fill leadership positions. Empirical research findings suggest that leaders with high levels of moral reasoning are perceived to be more transformational than leaders with low moral reasoning. That being said, it would be prudent for organizations to measure moral reasoning, and levels of transformational dimensions related to ethical leadership, in leadership candidates prior to hire.

Conclusion

This literature review defined, compared, and evaluated characteristics associated with transformational leadership and ethical leadership. Theory was substantiated with empirical findings. It is certain that ethical misconduct affects not only the organization, but also organizational members, customers, and stakeholders. Unethical decision making creates invisible barriers that hinder the organic functioning of an organization and, if unchecked, could lead to entropy. Further, empirical studies have lent additional insight as to how followers perceive transformational leaders, and how various characteristics of transformational leadership are related to context (i.e., cultural norms for tribute and nepotism). The antecedents for ethical organizational behavior do not lie only in the type of leadership style exhibited (although there is a clear case made for transformational leadership), but lie within the context of the organizational situation and within each person's value set. That being said, perhaps we should not ask whether leaders are considered ethical because they are transformational . . . or transformational because they are ethical. Instead, the appropriate question might be which of these forms of leadership has the most potential for fostering organizational ethical behavior and positive ethical outcomes.

Acknowledgements

The author thanks Jan Kottke for her generous time in thoughtful reviews of earlier versions of this manuscript, and Nancy Huber for providing constructive feedback and recommendations that enhanced this manuscript. In addition, the author expresses profound appreciation to Jean Lipman-Blumen for her mentorship.

REFERENCES

Aronson, E. (2001). Integrating leadership styles and ethical perspectives. *Canadian Journal of Administrative Science, 18*(4), 244–256.

Banerji, P., & Krishnan, V. R. (2000). Ethical preferences of transformational leaders: An empirical investigation. *Leadership and Organization Development Journal, 21*(8), 405–413.

Bartels, R. (1967). A model for ethics in marketing. *Journal of Marketing, 31*, 20–26.

Bartholomew, C. S., & Gustafson, S. B. (1998). Perceived Leader Integrity Scale: An instrument for assessing employee perceptions of leader integrity. *Leadership Quarterly, 9*(2), 127–145.

Bass, B. M. (1985). *Leadership and performance beyond expectations.* New York: Free Press.

Bass, B. M., & Steidlmeier, P. S. (1999). Ethics, character, and authentic transformational leadership behavior. *Leadership Quarterly, 10*(2), 181–217.

Bass, B. M., & Avolio, B. (1995). *MLQ Multifactor Leadership Questionnaire for research.* Redwood City, CA: Mindgarden.

Brown, M. E., & Treviño, L. K. (2006). Ethical leadership: A review and future directions. *Leadership Quarterly, 17*, 595–616.

Burns, J. M. (1978). *Leadership.* New York: Harper & Row.

Cohan, J. A. (2002). "I didn't know" and "I was only doing my job": Has corporate governance careened out of control? A case study of Enron's information myopia. *Journal of Business Ethics, 40*(3), 275–299.

Conger, J. A. (1999). Charismatic and transformational leadership in organizations: An insider's perspective on these developing streams of research. *Leadership Quarterly, 10*, 145–179.

Conger, J. A., & Kanungo, R. N. (1998). *Charismatic leadership in organizations.* Thousand Oaks, CA: Sage Publications.

Goldberg, L. R. (1990). An alternative "description of personality": The Big-Five factor structure. *Journal of Personality and Social Psychology, 59*(6), 1216–1229.

Hunt, S. D., & Vitell, S. (1986). A general theory of marketing ethics. *Journal of MacroMarketing, 8*, 5–16.

Kanungo, R. N. (2001). Ethical values of transactional and transformational leaders. *Canadian Journal of Administrative Sciences, 18*(4), 257–265.

Lipman-Blumen, J. (2005). *The allure of toxic leaders: Why we follow destructive bosses and corrupt politicians—and how we can survive them.* New York: Oxford University Press.

Margaret, J. (2003). Leadership style and its relationship to individual differences in personality, moral orientation, and ethical judgment—a PhD proposal. *Journal of American Academy of Business, 3,* 104–113.

McDonald, G., & Nijhof, A. (1999). Beyond codes of ethics: An integrated framework for stimulating morally responsible behaviour in organisations. *Leadership and Organization Development Journal, 20*(3), 133–146.

Mendonca, M. (2001). Preparing for ethical leadership in organizations. *Canadian Journal of Administrative Sciences, 18*(4), 266–276.

Minkes, A. L., Small, M. W., & Chatterjee, S. R. (1999). Leadership and business ethics: Does it matter? Implications for management. *Journal of Business Ethics, 20*(4), 327–335.

Moberg, D. J. (1999). The Big Five and organizational virtue. *Business Ethics Quarterly, 9*(2), 245–272.

Paine, L., Deshpandé, R., Margolis, J. D., & Bettcher, K. E. (2005). Up to code: Does your company's conduct meet world-class standards? *Harvard Business Review, 38*(12), 122–133.

Parry, K. W., & Proctor-Thomson, S. B. (2002). Perceived integrity of transformational leaders in organisational settings. *Journal of Business Ethics, 35*(2), 75–96.

Pelletier, K. L., & Bligh, M. C. (2006). Rebounding from corruption: Perceptions of ethics program effectiveness in a public sector organization. *Journal of Business Ethics, 67*(4), 359–374.

Rest, J. R. (1979). *Development in judging moral issues.* Minneapolis: University of Minnesota Press.

Schwartz, B. I. (1985). *The world of thought in ancient China.* Cambridge, MA: Belknap Press of Harvard University Press.

Schwarz, M. (2001). The nature of the relationship between corporate codes of ethics and behaviour. *Journal of Business Ethics, 32*(3), 247–262.

Singer, M. S., & Singer, A. E. (1997). Observer judgements about moral agents' ethical decisions: The role of scope of justice and moral intensity. *Journal of Business Ethics, 16*(5), 473–484.

Treddenick, H. (Trans.). (1969). *The apology of Plato.* New York: Penguin Books.

Turner, N., Barling, J., Epitropaki, O., Butcher, V., & Milner, C. (2002). Transformational leadership and moral reasoning. *Journal of Applied Psychology, 87*(2), 304–311.

KATHIE L. PELLETIER is a doctoral candidate at Claremont Graduate University in the School of Behavioral and Organizational Sciences. Her research interests include toxic and ethical leadership, organizational corruption, and women's issues in the workplace. She received her BA from San Diego State University and her MS in industrial/organizational psychology from California State University, San Bernardino. She is currently working with Dr. Jean Lipman-Blumen at the Achieving Styles Institute and is also an adjunct faculty member at California State University, San Bernardino.

Social Enterprise
Leadership, Climate, and Organizational Sustainability

By Virginia Klamon

Millions of children [are] dying every year in poor countries from diseases that we had long ago made harmless in this country. . . . The market did not reward saving the lives of these children, and governments did not subsidize it. . . . We can make market forces work better for the poor if we can develop a more creative capitalism.

Bill Gates (2007)

THE DEMANDS OF THIS CENTURY COMPEL US TO ENVISION A FUTURE where the bottom line stands in service to social good, not to competition. While the profit motive has significantly shaped the language and practice of business and bounded the interpretative frame of entrepreneurship, a profoundly new form of entrepreneurial organization is emerging, the social enterprise. Inspired by social purpose and fuelled by entrepreneurial drive, social enterprises leverage commercial success to achieve social justice (Alter, 2004; Emerson, 2000; Social Enterprise Coalition, 2003). Social entrepreneurs are reimagining the capitalist paradigm, reinventing the field of entrepreneurship, and redefining the social sector in promising new ways. Whether by pioneering the business of micro-lending, distributing fair-trade products, or employing at-risk adults, social entrepreneurs are passionate about addressing otherwise unmet societal needs. They work at the market fringe, targeting gaps where public service and private markets fail to deliver critical goods and services, particularly for those most marginalized by society (Drayton, 2002; Hartigan, 2004).

Social entrepreneurs focus their entrepreneurial talent on solving social problems such as why children are not learning or why technology is not equally accessed (Drayton, 2002). In doing so they face the critical challenge of entrepreneurship—transforming individual drive into collective purpose and commitment (Pettigrew, 1979). In attempting to master this transformation leaders have learned that dictating vision, no matter how heartfelt, is counterproductive (Block, 1993; Senge, 1990). The command-and-control model of leadership inhibits people from working together in meaningful ways and is out of step with the requirements of our evolving world marketplace (Wheatley, 1999).

> ❝ **SOCIAL ENTREPRENEURS ARE PASSIONATE ABOUT ADDRESSING OTHERWISE UNMET SOCIETAL NEEDS.** ❞

Can entrepreneurs achieve organizational results while attending to the human dimension? Robert Greenleaf (1970, 1977) argued that this paradox of leadership—results *with* respect—is reconciled through the concept of service. In introducing a theory of servant-leadership, Greenleaf intentionally applied the philosophy of service to the practice of leadership. He articulated this through his vocabulary of *servant as leader* and *servant as organization*. Greenleaf encouraged individuals to be custodians of society.

The practice of servant leadership nurtures autonomy and self-responsibility by cultivating critical-thinking skills, expanding capacity for moral reasoning, and enhancing participative competence (Graham, 1991). When organizational members participate in the expression of servant-leadership, they co-create a lived experience of "servanthood." In theory, what renders servant-leadership akin to social entrepreneurship is the ethical motivation that inspires individuals to act. In practice, questions remain.

This research introduced the lens of "organizational climate for servanthood" to examine whether two intriguing and emerging phenomena, servant-leadership and social entrepreneurism, intersect to create a healthy sustainable workplace. This study is the first to examine the interior life space of social enterprises. The findings provide significant insight into the social enterprise workplace experience.

Literature Review

This study draws together three theoretical models: (1) social entrepreneurship and enterprise, (2) organizational climate, and (3) servanthood, an organizational expression of servant-leadership. This first subsection reviews the emerging field of social entrepreneurship and social enterprise models. The following subsection highlights the organizational climate and culture literatures. The third subsection presents servant-leadership, specifically the defining attributes of servanthood, and the servanthood climate survey instrument.

Emerging Field of Social Entrepreneurship

Martin (2004) classifies the two most prominent emerging schools of thought on social entrepreneurship as "individualist" and "contextualist." As Martin describes, individualists tend to focus on traits that distinguish social entrepreneurs from business entrepreneurs or from other social agents. Contextualists acknowledge social entrepreneurship as a phenomenon rising in the midst of recent globalization.

According to Martin (2004), the contextualist story unfolds in the late 1980s when Bill Drayton founded Ashoka, an organization dedicated to developing the profession of social entrepreneurship by shaping a citizen sector that is entrepreneurial, productive, and globally integrated (Ashoka, 2005). Drayton traveled the world in search of individuals using innovative methods for advancing social change. Through Ashoka, Drayton assembled a global fellowship of social entrepreneurs and created a thriving social innovation community of practice. In the ensuing years, the social entrepreneurship movement drew wider public attention as citizens became increasingly aware of exploding social and economic inequality occurring in the world. Corporate social responsibility and citizenship agendas emerged in parallel, largely motivated by anti-globalization sentiment and heightened media attention on social issues. Alongside these events, the rising legitimacy of commercial entrepreneurship stimulated a new enterprising model.

" CAN ENTREPRENEURS ACHIEVE ORGANIZATIONAL " RESULTS WHILE ATTENDING TO THE HUMAN DIMENSION?

Present-day social entrepreneurs are constructing a radical new worldview that combines social activism with business discipline (Drayton, 2002; Fourth Sector Network, 2006). Mainstream news journals, business periodicals, and television broadcasts now feature the work of social entrepreneurs' visionary enterprises. Recent headlines include 2006 Nobel Peace Prize winner Muhammad Yunus of Grameen Bank, and Jordan Kassalow of New York-based Scojo Foundation.

Three overarching perspectives characterize the variations in contemporary social entrepreneurship applications (Alvord, Brown, & Letts, 2002). One view holds that social entrepreneurship is a vehicle to catalyze large-scale social transformation (Ashoka, 2005). A second perspective describes social entrepreneurship as innovating for social impact. Innovations and social arrangements are the key mechanisms to advance social change, and little emphasis is placed on commercial viability (Dees, 2001). A third perspective defines social entrepreneurship as the combination of commercial enterprise with social outcomes. Often the organizing form takes the shape of social enterprise. From this view, social entrepreneurship is "the art of persistently and creatively leveraging resources to capitalize upon marketplace opportunities in order to achieve sustainable social change" (Social Enterprise Alliance, 2004).

Social Enterprise

As depicted in Figure 1, organizations may be distinguished from one another according to their business purpose and conceptually aligned along a spectrum of motives (Alter, 2004; Emerson, 2000). As Dees (1996) outlines, purely philanthropic organizations that serve the public interest and solely rely on capital, labor, and in-kind donations (e.g., church pantry) anchor one end of the spectrum. Purely commercial enterprises that operate in a rational self-regarding interest, and exchange goods, services, and payments through economic markets, anchor the opposing end. Hybrid organizations operate in the middle ground between purely philanthropic and commercial enterprises and serve differing aspects of both social and commercial value creation. A social enterprise is but one of four different hybrid organizations that uses a blend of market and mission-driven methods to achieve social impact (see Figure 1). Hybrid organizations adjacent to social enterprises include nonprofit organizations with income-generating activities and socially responsible businesses.

The legal structure of a social enterprise varies, but nonprofit status is more common than a for-profit structure. Distinguishing between a nonprofit social enterprise and a nonprofit organization with income-generating activities is subtle and subject to debate (Alter, 2004). Alter argues that income-generating activities, when

Figure 1. Spectrum of Hybrid Organizations

Adapted from *Social Enterprise Typology* by K. Alter (2004, p. 7).

operated as a business, differentiate social enterprises from other nonprofit organizations. Dees (2005) augments this definition, incorporating a requirement for entrepreneurial and innovative methods for creating social change. For this reason, nonprofit hospitals and other similar nonprofit institutions are classified as nonprofit income-generating organizations, not social enterprises (Dees, 1996). Innovative methods for delivering against a social mission, supported by entrepreneurial self-financing activity, render social enterprise unique.

Entrepreneurship scholars and practitioners are becoming increasingly particular about making these attributes requisite components of the social enterprise construct (Boschee & McClurg, 2003; Dees, 2005). This is due in part to honor the remarkable contributions of social entrepreneurs and to call attention to the risk of endorsing exaggerated claims absent evidence of fundamental change (Boschee & McClurg, 2003).

❝   **PRESENT-DAY SOCIAL ENTREPRENEURS ARE**   **❞**
CONSTRUCTING A RADICAL NEW WORLDVIEW
THAT COMBINES SOCIAL ACTIVISM WITH BUSINESS
DISCIPLINE.

A socially responsible business, situated on the commercial end of the spectrum, serves a primary goal of economic value in a way that respects ethical values, people, communities, and the environment (Dees & Anderson, 2003). Notable examples of this type of hybrid organization include Ben and Jerry's and The Body Shop. Emerson (2004) claims "the work of social entrepreneurship and the creation of social enterprise is also the work of a for-profit manager striving to drive the practice of corporate social responsibility into her firm" (p. viii). Hence, a corporation with socially responsible business practices constitutes the fourth hybrid form. These businesses typically achieve social impact through the work of their corporate foundations or employee volunteer activities.

Organizational Climate and Culture

Culture determines individuals' orientations to one another, to their work, and to their environment; climate unfolds as individuals experience these orientations through actions and interpretations (Michela & Burke, 2000). The degree to which the cultural phenomenon is visible depends on the level at which it is manifest, ranging from tangible expressions to unconscious assumptions (Schein, 1992). Behavior and espoused values comprise the surface and intermediate levels of organizational culture (Schein, 1992), which are measurable through the construct of climate (Denison,

1990). Deeper levels of organizational culture are characterized by the pattern of shared beliefs held by organizational members. These shared meanings and assumptions are largely tacit, particular to a group or subgroup, and create some level of structural stability within a group (Louis, 1980; Morgan, 1986; Schein, 1992).

Organizational climate can be described as "configurations of attitudes and perceptions by organization members, that, in combination, reflect a substantial part of the context of which they are a part and within which they work" (Ashkanasy, Wilderom, & Peterson, 2000, p. 8). Climate is perceptible through a myriad of overt expressions often evident in daily organizational life, including rituals, ceremonies, language, and dress (Schein, 1992). Climate describes how members experience their organizations by measuring their perceptions of their workplace (Koys & DeCotiis, 1991).

The most basic characteristic of an organizational climate index is its referent, the organization (Denison, 1990, 1996). As a theoretical model, organizational climate is a unit-level construct with shared unit properties; the properties originate in the individual unit members' experiences, attitudes, and perceptions and emerge as a consensual, collective aspect of the unit as a whole (Kozlowski & Klein, 2000). The aggregation of lower-level variables into higher-level variables creates an aggregate-level construct that is both related to and different from its lower-level counterpart; it is partially isomorphic (Bliese, 2000). Bliese refers to this aggregation as a "fuzzy composition process." Agreement and reliability indices play an important role in establishing construct validity of a climate model, and are particularly relevant in detecting emerging phenomena (Bliese, 2000).

Servant-Leadership: A Construct of Servanthood

Servant-leadership requires new terms of engagement between individuals in a leadership relationship. This philosophy calls each member to be personally accountable for the success of a group or organization, dispersing responsibility throughout the organization. Robert Greenleaf's (1970, 1977, 1996) inspired servant-leadership writings only began to materially circulate among leadership scholars and practitioners since the 1990s. Mainstreaming this literature has been a slow process. Although Greenleaf was a lifelong business practitioner, he articulated his servant-leadership philosophy as a conceptual framework, rendering its application difficult (Northouse, 2001). His focus was the consequential impact of servant-leaders' actions on others and the institutional environments in which they worked. He positioned servant-leadership outcomes as the ultimate test for effectiveness. Leadership theories often espouse effectiveness, yet few define the measure by which it is evaluated. The performance measure for servant-leadership is whether those served grow as individuals and whether they become healthier, wiser, more autonomous, and likely to serve others (Spears, 1995).

Although scholars, business leaders, and organizational consultants claim that servant-leadership core concepts are essential prescriptions for the twenty-first-century organization (Bennis & Nanus, 1998; Block, 1993; Drucker, 1999; Jaworski, 1996; Wheatley, 1999; Zohar, 1997), few tools exist that operationalize and measure this construct. A review of the literature identified only three research instruments that explicitly target servant-leadership in an organizational context. Abel (2000) identified the work environments in which servant-leaders are effective or ineffective. However, Abel's theory of workplace effectiveness focused exclusively on the servant-leader cohort in the context of the environment, and empirical validation was not conducted. Ehrhart (2001) developed a general measure of servant-leadership based solely on a literature review and validated by a field test consisting of 254 university students averaging nineteen years of age with limited work experience. Furthermore, he defined leadership as a "unit-level cognition about how unit members as a whole are treated by the leader" (p. 36). This definition overlooks the reciprocal and relational nature of social exchange in the servant-leadership paradigm.

Laub (1999) constructed a survey instrument, the Organizational Leadership Assessment (OLA), based on a Delphi process consisting of fourteen servant-leadership experts. The OLA was designed as a comprehensive model of servant-leadership applied to organizational life. The OLA examines the distributed aspects of leadership and servanthood by measuring perceptions across all organizational levels. It is a proven valid and reliable instrument with strong construct and face validity (Laub, 1999, 2003). In operationalizing the servant-leadership philosophy, six dimensions emerged as key characteristics: (1) values others, (2) develops others, (3) builds community, (4) displays authenticity, (5) provides leadership, and (6) shares leadership (Laub, 1999). These six dimensions underpinned this research study.

The OLA instrument intentionally employs common use vocabulary to facilitate ease of understanding. The instrument is sectioned into three parts, measuring the respondent's perceptions of: (1) a generalized view of all organizational members, (2) a generalized view of all executive leaders/directors, managers, and supervisors, and (3) his/her direct relationship with his/her leader(s). The data may be analyzed at the organization or organizational subgroup level.

Research Methodology and Sample Description

This study was designed as exploratory research, employing a survey method based on nonprobability sampling. The OLA survey instrument supported the introduction of the multilevel climate for servanthood construct, aligning theory with measurement. The OLA is consistent with the protocol requirements for organizational climate instruments, specifically: (a) use of nonevaluative, nonobjective measures; (b) data are perception-based and amenable to analysis at various levels; (c) dimensions are theoretically sound; (d) items target an issue of interest; and (e) items describe facets of the organizational experience/environment, exclusive of organizational structure (Koys & DeCotiis, 1991; Newman, 1977; Schneider, 1975). The OLA was a superior choice for use in this study based on Laub's (1999) Delphi process, its strong psychometric properties, the extensive field test, and the instrument's subsequent use in numerous research studies.

To address the research questions of this study and to gain a better understanding of the variables and their relationships, descriptive statistics, intraclass correlations, and estimates of agreement and reliability were run. Social enterprise OLA results were compared to prior OLA research results. Within-group agreement was calculated using alternative variants of the r_{wg} statistic (James, Demaree, & Wolf, 1993; Lindell, 2001; Lindell, Brandt, & Whitney, 1999). A one-way random-effects ANOVA was used to calculate reliability in both of the two major forms of the intraclass correlation coefficient, the ICC(1) and ICC(2) (Bliese, 2000).

Thought and practice leaders in the social enterprise domain recommended organizations to include in the sample. Each expert was asked to provide at least five recommendations based on sample selection criteria that included: (a) the study definition of social enterprise; (b) a geographic region defined as the United States of America; and (c) a requisite number of organizational members (i.e., employees and volunteers) totaling at least ten individuals. Some individuals suggested additional field experts and provided email addresses to facilitate direct inquiry. Twenty social enterprise organizations agreed to participate in the study from the sample frame of forty-nine enterprises. Of the twenty participating organizations, sixteen provided usable data. Results were based on 208 surveys collected from these sixteen social enterprises located throughout the United States and in Canada.

The survey, conducted via the Internet, ran from September 21 to October 17, 2005, on a 24x7 schedule. WebSurveyor® Corporation, an independent commercial application service provider, hosted the survey site, capturing data via secure and confidential electronic methods. Organizational demographic information was collected from each participating social enterprise. These organizational data included: social enterprise business area, year founded, total FTEs, tax status, total budget, and social enterprise profitability status (see Table 1).

In addition to the organizational information collected, five personal demographic questions were asked of the survey respondents. Specifically, the questions inquired about respondents' organizational role and tenure, gender, education, and

Table 1. Social Enterprise Organizational Demographic Data

Variable	Category	N	Percentages	n	Percentages
Business Area	Education	1	6.3	25	11.9
	Environment/Animals	1	6.3	6	2.9
	Health	2	12.5	13	6.2
	Human Services	5	31.3	100	48.1
	Public/Society Benefit	2	12.5	11	5.2
	Other	5	31.3	53	25.7
	Total	16	100.0	208	100.0
Year Founded	Before 1990	4	25.0	98	47.1
	1990 – 1999	6	37.5	46	22.1
	2000 – 2005	6	37.5	64	30.8
	Total	16	100.0	208	100.0
FTEs	0–9 FTEs	6	37.5	49	23.3
	10–19 FTEs	6	37.5	50	24.3
	20–39 FTEs	2	12.5	30	14.3
	> 40 FTEs	2	12.5	79	38.1
	Total	16	100.0	208	100.0
Tax Status	Nonprofit	15	93.7	196	94.3
	For-Profit	1	6.3	12	5.7
	Total	16	100.0	208	100.0
Operating Budget	< $499,999	4	25.0	30	14.3
	$500,000 – $2.4 million	6	37.5	46	22.4
	> $2.5 million	6	37.5	132	63.3
	Total	16	100.0	208	100.0
Profit Status	Requires Subsidy	5	31.2	40	19.0
	Breakeven	4	25.0	29	14.3
	Financial Surplus	3	18.7	80	38.1
	Uncertain	1	6.3	5	2.4
	Other	3	18.7	54	26.2
	Total	16	100.0	208	100.0

age. The survey required responses to all questions, but respondents could choose the option of "decline to answer" for age, gender, and education related questions.

The survey sample included 52.9% female, 38.1% male, and 9% declined to answer. Over half of the respondents (57.1%) completed undergraduate or graduate education. Of those providing an age, 43.8% were younger than forty and 45.2% were forty or older; 11% declined to answer. The majority of participants (69.5%) worked for the social enterprise three years or less, 18.2% worked between four to six years, and 12.3% had a tenure of seven years or greater. Overall, the sample consisted of: 21% Executive Leaders/Directors, 31.9% Managers/Supervisors, 37.6% Staff, 5.2% Board Members, and 3.3% Volunteers. One percent of organizational role data was missing.

This research study viewed climate and culture through the "Integration" frame (Martin, 2002) whereby perceptual consensus was necessary to justify aggregating data (George & James, 1993). When studying organizational climate it is important to show that group members agree in their perceptions of the workplace. Measurement indices must indicate that survey ratings are more similar to each other than would be expected by chance.

Climate-related agreement levels for the study enterprises ranged from moderate to high, and were accompanied by a considerable degree of respondent reliability. Therefore, survey responses could be justifiably aggregated for each study enterprise. Based on the aggregated average survey score, each enterprise was placed into one of the organizational climate and health categories. This study utilized the procedure for estimating agreement based on the indices presented by Lindell (2001). Findings from this exploratory study of social enterprise organizational climate may be used, with caution, to draw inferences about deeper levels of organizational culture.

Research Findings
Summary

To a considerable extent, enterprise members in this study created healthy, servant-oriented workplaces (see Figure 2). Based on the aggregated average survey score, each enterprise was placed into one of the organizational climate and health categories. Almost one half of the social enterprises (44%) in this sample met the OLA empirical requirements for servant organizations. An additional 12.5% were at the servant-paternal boundary, suggesting that they, too, materially share the attributes of healthy servant organizations. This finding provides an encouraging outlook for social enterprise organizational life, notably more positive than prior research investigating other workplace settings (Laub, 2003).

Servant organizations achieve and sustain the highest levels of organizational health (Laub, 2003). These organizations call forth the wisdom of their employees, contribute to their sense of greater purpose, and reinforce their personal and professional values in a manner that invites full participation, self-responsibility, and interdependence. In servant workplaces, failures are viewed as learning opportunities and creativity is both encouraged and rewarded.

Figure 2. Social Enterprise Results Summary

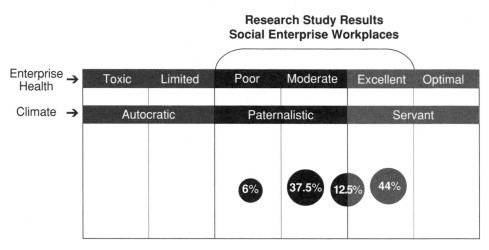

Research Study Results
Social Enterprise Workplaces

Enterprise Health →	Toxic	Limited	Poor	Moderate	Excellent	Optimal
Climate →	Autocratic		Paternalistic		Servant	
			6%	37.5% 12.5%	44%	

Adapted from "Six Organizational Health Level Descriptions," by J. Laub, in *The International Journal of Servant-Leadership,* 2005, p. 180.

No participating enterprises in this study enacted an autocratic climate—a marked contrast to the 31% autocratic organizations found in prior research (Laub, 2003). Still, the study results call for balanced optimism. Just over one-third of the study enterprises (37.5%) created a positively paternalistic climate, and a further 6% enacted a negatively paternalistic climate. Members' perceptions about their workplace were generally more diverse in paternalistic versus servant enterprises, reflecting differing views about their organizational experience. In paternalistic enterprises, organizational trust is more fragile, leaving some members uncertain about just how open they can be with one another (Laub, 2003). In these workplaces risks may be taken, but there is an underlying fear of failure. Paternalistic leadership embeds the tacit assumption that leaders are wiser and more knowledgeable than followers (Wong, 2003). Members come to rely on leaders for guidance and decision making, which inhibits individual and organizational maturation and ultimately jeopardizes long-term enterprise sustainability.

In positively paternalistic environments where organizational health is moderate (Laub, 2003), reward power may be used to establish member loyalty (Wong, 2003). Leaders value relationships when they benefit organizational goals, but task execution is the first priority. Furthermore, members may experience tension stemming from an implicit expectation of conformity instead of open acceptance of diversity. In negatively paternalistic environments, conformity is expected and individual expression is discouraged (Laub, 2003). Members are valued more for their contribution and less for who they are, and teams tend to display competitive energy versus collaborative behaviors. Generally, this is a noticeably individualist environment with limited organizational health.

Detailed Findings and Practitioner Implications

Over one half of the survey questions (55%) gathered perceptions about executive leaders and directors, those individuals who hold formal authority in their organizations. Interestingly, though, on average survey ratings were lower on questions about leader behavior versus questions pertaining to all members or questions specific to the respondents (see Figure 3). In other words, respondents' perceptions indicated that the entire community of organizational members demonstrated characteristics of servant-leadership to a greater extent than the social enterprise leader cohort. This outcome acknowledges the central role organizational members play in shaping climate and culture, and simultaneously draws attention to the opportunity for social enterprise leaders to more fully demonstrate servant-leadership behaviors.

Respondents perceived their personal relationship with their leaders more positively than they viewed all leaders in general (see Figure 3). Several survey questions explored respondents' perceptions about their personal role in the organization. For example, questions inquired whether respondents personally felt appreciated, listened to, and affirmed by those above them. The results suggest either that individuals experienced servanthood behaviors more consistently in the interpersonal interaction with their bosses, or that individuals were less familiar with other organizational leaders and therefore unable to comment on the presence of the targeted behaviors, resulting in a neutral rating score.

Further patterns emerged from the six servant-leadership dimensions (see Figure 4). *Builds communities* and *displays authenticity* moved upward in servant-oriented enterprises, marking these characteristics more distinctive among the servant-leadership dimensions. In contrast, *displays authenticity* received one of the lowest scores of all subscales in the negatively paternalistic environment. Perceptions related to *provides leadership* moved downward in servant and positively paternalistic environments, while they increased in the negatively paternalistic workplace. This upward movement suggests that members perceived clarity of direction, goal definition, and accountability with greater emphasis (relative to other dimensions) in the negatively paternalistic organization than in servant or positively paternalistic enterprises. This may be a signal that respondents in servant-oriented and positively paternalistic environments look for more focused direction from their leaders.

Figure 3. Survey Subgroup Perceptions

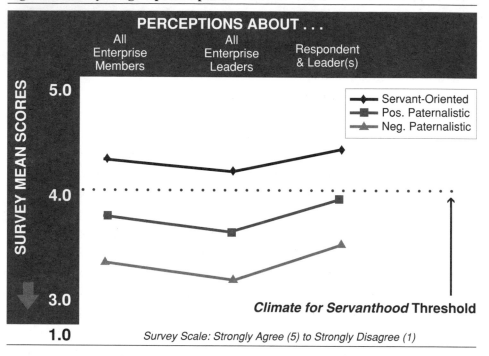

Figure 4. Servant-Leadership Dimension Results

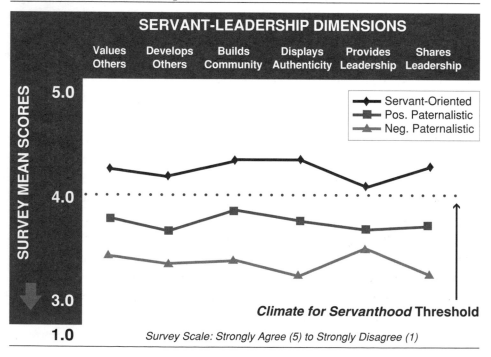

Builds communities was a distinguishing feature of servant-oriented social enterprises. Although with approximately half the study enterprises classified as paternalistic, there exists an opportunity for social enterprises to more actively foster the organizational conditions that nurture relationships and catalyze the emergence of productive enterprise communities.

While survey respondents in servant-oriented social enterprises perceived a notable presence of authentic behavior, perceptions in paternalistic workplaces trended downward. These results highlight the opportunity to foster deeper levels of authenticity among enterprise members and specifically among leaders. Similar to *builds communities*, members in servant-oriented enterprises scored *displays authenticity* among the highest dimensions (refer to Figure 4). The survey emphasizes the personal characteristics of integrity, honesty, and trustworthiness. The questions specifically draw attention to whether leaders are open to learning from others, able to constructively receive criticism, and voluntarily admit mistakes. When individuals create a negatively paternalistic climate, advancing from limited organizational health to a more productive climate requires profound transformation.

The assessed dimensions of *provides leadership* and *shares leadership* were inversely related when comparing servant-oriented and negatively paternalistic climates (refer to Figure 4). It is both possible and desirable to empower others while providing direction. As scholars similarly point out, organizations perform best when individuals are adaptive, yet highly consistent and predictable, and foster high involvement but do so within the context of a shared vision (Denison & Mishra, 1995). In practice, social enterprise leaders may struggle in expressing *provides leadership* and *shares leadership* behaviors as complementary. Strikingly, members in servant-oriented and positively paternalistic enterprises scored *provides leadership* among the lowest dimension, yet *shares leadership* was scored relatively high. In contrast, members in the negatively paternalistic enterprise scored *provides leadership* as the highest subscale and *shares leadership* among the lowest. Social enterprise leaders would benefit by developing a more balanced expression of *provides leadership* and *shares leadership*.

Lastly, a gap existed between knowing who others are and acting on the capacity to support who they want to become. This finding suggests a possible "knowing-doing" gap. In general, members perceived a higher level of *valuing* versus *developing* behaviors. This scored relationship, between *values others* and *develops others,* was similar in all enterprise climates (refer to Figure 4). Notably, in both servant-oriented and positively paternalistic enterprises, members' perceptions of *develops others* measured among the lowest. Social enterprise members, and particularly leaders, may benefit from developing coaching and mentoring skills so they can, in turn, facilitate the development of others.

 SOCIAL ENTERPRISE MEMBERS, AND PARTICULARLY LEADERS, MAY BENEFIT FROM DEVELOPING COACHING AND MENTORING SKILLS.

Directions for Future Research

As with all empirical research, certain limitations were associated with this study. First, a nonrandom and restricted sample size limited this research. Second, since this study pioneered exploration of the social enterprise workplace experience, a lack of comparative data constrained interpretive analysis. Finally, OLA research using the Autocratic-Paternalistic-Servant model of organizational health is nascent and OLA norm group data are limited. This study also introduced new measurement methods for OLA research, and comparative data from multi-organization OLA studies do not exist.

This study was the first to examine the interior life space of social enterprises. Additional research is needed to more broadly characterize the enterprise workplace experience. Future directions for research include replicating this study but increasing the number of social enterprises with a particular focus on diversifying enterprise size and age demographics. Qualitative research to experientially investigate the lived organizational practices in social enterprises would also be beneficial, since individuals may respond to survey questions based on idealized perceptions of behavior. Finally, whether servant enterprises demonstrate higher levels of organizational performance is uncertain, presenting another interesting area for further study.

REFERENCES

Abel, A. T. (2000). *The characteristics, behaviors, and effective work environments of servant leaders: A Delphi study.* Unpublished doctoral dissertation, Virginia Polytechnic Institute and State University, Blacksburg, VA.

Alter, K. (2004). *Social enterprise typology.* Retrieved September 20, 2004, from http://www.virtueventures.com/setypology.pdf

Alvord, S. H., Brown, L. D., & Letts, C. W. (2002). Social entrepreneurship: Leadership that facilitates societal transformation—An exploratory study (Working Paper 3). Retrieved April 8, 2005, from http://www.ksg.harvard.edu/leadership/Pdf/AlvordBrownLettsWorkingPaper.pdf

Ashkanasy, N. M., Wilderom, C. P. M., & Peterson, M. F. (2000). *Handbook of organizational culture and climate.* Thousand Oaks, CA: Sage Publications.

Ashoka. (2005). *Ashoka's mission.* Retrieved May 19, 2005, from http://www.ashoka.org/what_is/mission.cfm

Bennis, W., & Nanus, B. (1998). Toward the new millennium. In G. R. Hickman (Ed.), *Leading organizations: Perspectives for a new era* (pp. 5–7). Thousand Oaks, CA: Sage Publications.

Bliese, P. (2000). Within-group agreement, non-independence, and reliability: Implications for data aggregation and analysis. In K. Klein & S. Kozlowski (Eds.), *Multilevel theory, research, and methods in organizations* (pp. 349–381). San Francisco: Jossey-Bass.

Block, P. (1993). *Stewardship: Choosing service over self-interest.* San Francisco: Berrett-Koehler.

Boschee, J., & McClurg, J. (2003). *Toward a better understanding of social entrepreneurship: Some important distinctions.* Unpublished manuscript.

Dees, J. G. (1996). *The social enterprise spectrum: Philanthropy to commerce.* Cambridge, MA: Harvard Business School Publishing.

Dees, J. G. (2001). *The meaning of social entrepreneurship.* Retrieved July 10, 2004, from http://www.sbs.ox.ac.uk/html/faculty_skoll_entrepren.asp#definition

Dees, J. G. (2005). *ConnectCASE newsletter.* Retrieved January 26, 2005, from http://www.fuqua.duke.edu/centers/case/about/news.html

Dees, J. G., & Anderson, B. B. (2003). For-profit social ventures. *International Journal of Entrepreneurship Education, 2,* 1–26.

Denison, D. R. (1990). *Corporate culture and organizational effectiveness.* New York: John Wiley & Sons.

Denison, D. R. (1996). What is the difference between organizational culture and organizational climate? A native's point of view on a decade of paradigm wars. *Academy of Management Review, 21*(3), 619–654.

Denison, D. R., & Mishra, A. K. (1995). Toward a theory of organizational culture and effectiveness. *Organization Science, 6*(2), 204–223.

Drayton, W. (2002). The citizen sector: Becoming as entrepreneurial and competitive as business. *California Management Review, 44*(3), 120–133.

Drucker, P. F. (1999). The discipline of innovation. In F. Hesselbein & P. M. Cohen (Eds.), *Leader to leader: Enduring insights on leadership from the Drucker Foundation's award winning journal* (pp. 53–56). San Francisco: Jossey-Bass.

Emerson, J. (2000). *The nature of returns: A social capital markets inquiry into elements of investment and the blended value proposition* (Social Enterprise Series Working Paper 17). Boston: Harvard Business School.

Emerson, J. (2004). Foreword. In K. Alter, *Social enterprise typology* (pp. vi–viii). Retrieved September 20, 2004, from http://www.virtueventures.com/setypology.pdf

Ehrhart, M. G. (2001). *Leadership and justice climate as antecedents of unit-level organizational citizenship behavior.* Unpublished doctoral dissertation, University of Maryland, College Park, MD.

Fourth Sector Network. (2006). *Home page.* Retrieved May 9, 2006, from www.fourthsector.net

Gates, B. (2007) *Newsroom speeches and commentary page.* Retrieved July 25, 2007, from http://www.gatesfoundation.org/MediaCenter/Speeches/Co-ChairSpeeches/BillgSpeeches/BGSpeechHarvard-070607.htm

George, J., & James, L. (1993). Personality, affect, and behavior in groups revisited: Comment on aggregation, levels of analysis, and a recent application of within and between analysis. *Journal of Applied Psychology, 78*(5), 798–804.

Graham, J. (1991). Servant-leadership in organizations: Inspirational and moral. *Leadership Quarterly, 2*(2), 105–119.

Greenleaf, R. K. (1970). *The servant as leader.* Indianapolis, IN: Robert K. Greenleaf Center.

Greenleaf, R. K. (1977). *Servant leadership: A journey into the nature of legitimate power and greatness.* New York: Paulist Press.

Greenleaf, R. K. (1996). *On becoming a servant leader*. San Francisco: Jossey-Bass.

Hartigan, P. (2004). The challenge for social entrepreneurship. *Global Summit 2004*. Retrieved February 17, 2005, from http://www.schwabfound.org/news.htm?sid=10

James, L. R., Demaree, R. G., & Wolf, G. (1993). An assessment of within-group interrater agreement. *Journal of Applied Psychology, 78*(2), 306–309.

Jaworski, J. (1996). *Synchronicity: The inner path of leadership*. San Francisco: Berrett-Koehler.

Koys, D. J., & DeCotiis, T. A. (1991). Inductive measures of psychological climate. *Human Relations, 44*(3), 265–285.

Kozlowski, S., & Klein, K. (2000). A multilevel approach to theory and research in organizations: Contextual, temporal, and emergent processes. In K. Klein & S. Kozlowski (Eds.), *Multilevel theory, research, and methods in organizations* (pp. 3–90). San Francisco: Jossey-Bass.

Laub, J. (1999). *Assessing the servant organization: Development of the servant organizational leadership assessment (SOLA) instrument*. Unpublished doctoral dissertation, Florida Atlantic University, Boca Raton.

Laub, J. (2003). *From paternalism to the servant organization: Expanding the Organizational Leadership Assessment (OLA) model*. Paper presented at the Servant Leadership Roundtable at Regent University, Virginia Beach, VA.

Lindell, M. K. (2001). Assessing and testing interrater agreement on a single target using multi-item rating scales. *Applied Psychological Measurement, 25*(1), 89–99.

Lindell, M., Brandt, C., & Whitney, D. (1999). A revised index of interrater agreement for multi-item ratings of a single target. *Applied Psychological Measurement, 23*(2), 127–135.

Louis, M. R. (1980). Surprise and sense making: What newcomers experience in entering unfamiliar organizational settings. *Administrative Science Quarterly, 25*(2), 226–251.

Martin, J. (2002). *Organizational culture: Mapping the terrain*. Thousand Oaks, CA: Sage Publications.

Martin, M. (2004). *Surveying social entrepreneurship: Toward an empirical analysis of the performance revolution in the social sector* (Band 2). St, Gallen, Switzerland: University of St. Gallen, Center for Public Leadership.

Michela, J. L., & Burke, W. W. (2000). Organizational culture and climate in transformations for quality and innovation. In N. Ashkanasy, C. Wilderom, & M. Peterson (Eds.), *Handbook of organizational culture and climate* (pp. 225–244). Thousand Oaks, CA: Sage Publications.

Morgan, G. (1986). *Images of organizations*. Thousand Oaks, CA: Sage Publications.

Newman, J. (1977). Development of a measure of perceived work environment. *Academy of Management Journal, 20*(4), 520–534.

Northouse, P. (2001). *Leadership theory and practice*. Thousand Oaks, CA: Sage Publications.

Pettigrew, A. M. (1979). On studying organizational cultures. *Administrative Science Quarterly, 24*, 570–581.

Schein, E. H. (1992). *Organizational culture and leadership* (2nd ed.). San Francisco, CA: Jossey-Bass.

Schneider, B. (1975). Organizational climates: An essay. *Personal Psychology, 28*, 447–479.

Senge, P. M. (1990). *The fifth discipline: The art & practice of the learning organization*. New York: Currency Doubleday.

Social Enterprise Alliance. (2004). *Social enterprise lexicon*. Retrieved March 14, 2004, from http://www.se-alliance.org/resources_lexicon.cfm

Social Enterprise Coalition. (2003). *There's more to business than you think: A guide to social enterprise*. London: Social Enterprise Coalition.

Spears, L. C. (1995). *Reflections on leadership*. New York: John Wiley.

Wheatley, M. J. (1999). Good-bye, command and control. In F. Hesselbein & P. M. Cohen (Eds.), *Leader to leader: Enduring insights on leadership from the Drucker Foundation's award winning journal* (pp. 151–162). San Francisco: Jossey-Bass.

Wong, P. (2003). *An opponent-process model of servant-leadership and a typology of leadership styles*. Paper based on presentation at the Servant Leadership Roundtable at Regent University, Virginia Beach, VA.

Zohar, D. (1997). *Rewiring the corporate brain: Using the new science to rethink how we structure and lead organizations*. San Francisco: Berrett-Koehler.

VIRGINIA KLAMON is a practitioner-scholar dedicated to helping clients transform their workplaces into healthy, productive organizational communities. She has over twenty years of experience working in and consulting to organizations throughout North America and Europe. Through her research she explores the interrelationship between leadership and organizational culture. Virginia has a keen interest in social entrepreneurship and is committed to advancing the practice of social enterprise. She is active with Social Venture Partners International, a nonprofit venture philanthropy organization. She is a consulting member of the Society for Organizational Learning and founder of Zurich Leadership Network, a European-based learning community. She earned a PhD in leadership studies from Gonzaga University, and can be contacted via www.vklamon.com.

Leadership Dialogue
Interpersonal Communication Competence to Engage in Organizational Relationships

By Maijastiina Rouhiainen

THIS PAPER IS AN INVITATION TO A DIALOGUE ON LEADERSHIP DIAlogue. Three propositions on leadership communication are advanced: (1) leadership is fundamentally based on human interaction, (2) leadership is fundamentally dialogical, and (3) dialogue is part of leadership communication competence. The purpose of this study is to find out what kind of interpersonal communication competence is essential for leaders in a knowledge-based organization. In particular, the focus is on how leaders themselves conceptualize leadership communication competence and whether it is seen by leaders as innately dialogical.

The research topic is approached through a case study, namely through the opinions and experiences of work and the meanings given to human interaction practices in it of the leadership personnel in a research and development organization. Seventeen leaders in different management positions on all organizational levels were interviewed. The data gathered were analyzed qualitatively using the cross-case approach by Miles and Huberman (1994) and the constant comparative model of grounded theory by Strauss and Corbin (1990).

The findings of this study support in part the three propositions presented above about leadership communication and the dialogical nature of leadership. The approach offers insights into the interpersonal factors which lie at the core of leadership. The results offer a new perspective on leadership dialogue and leadership communication competence in a knowledge-based organization. Additionally, the interpersonal communication competence view of leadership serves as a basis for leadership training and development.

In a knowledge-based organization, where work is conceptual, abstract, and based on creating and sharing meanings, traditional ways of organizing and leading work are no longer valid. When knowledge arises out of the collaborative interaction between organizational members, administrative practice based on the principle of hierarchy seems an inappropriate way to lead. Instead, managers and leaders need to learn alternative principles for managing knowledge-based organizations and purposive work (see Heaton & Taylor, 2002, p. 232). In other words, in a knowledge-based organization purposive work value is created by human interaction that produces meaningful and collaborative social interaction. Leadership communication competence is one of the core factors in organizational success when leading such organization and work.

Although organizational and leadership communication competence have been investigated to some extent (e.g., Flauto, 1999; Jablin & Sias, 2001, pp. 821–827) and their importance is acknowledged (e.g., Fairhurst, 2001; Hackman & Johnson, 2004; Tourish & Hargie, 1999), little research has been conducted on leadership communication competence in the context of knowledge-based organizations and purposive work. There is a lack of information about the existing level of interpersonal communication competence of leaders and how it is understood.

As working life and organizations change, new theoretical understandings of communication and organization are needed (Taylor, Flanagin, Cheney, & Seibold, 2000, p. 115). This study presents three propositions on leadership, leadership communication, and leadership communication competence: (1) leadership is fundamentally based on human interaction, (2) leadership is fundamentally dialogical, and (3) dialogue is part of leadership communication competence. The existing research related to the three propositions is reviewed below.

Theoretical Background
Proposition 1: Leadership is fundamentally based on human interaction
Whereas in the past leadership communication research has been very leader-focused, recently there has been growing interest in the collective and interactive nature of leadership (Fairhurst, 2001, p. 379). Flanagin, Stohl, and Bimber (2006, pp. 31–32) suggest that in the contemporary organization, interaction between the organization's leaders and its members cannot be largely one-way and essentially prescribed; instead relational communication and high trust should be prioritized over more formal relations.

In this study, leadership communication competence is investigated through the work of the formal leadership personnel. However, leadership is not seen only as influencing others through leadership speech (monologue), but also as an interpersonal relationship (dialogue). When we conceptualize leadership through the concept of dialogue, we are stating that leadership communication is not only a function or a task, but a fundamental aspect of leadership. Communication is not simply a medium through which leadership happens to be exercised; it is part of its substance (Cohen, 2004, p. 177). As Barge (1994, p. 21) states, leadership emerges in the process of human interaction and is enacted through communication. Leadership occurs when a leader engages in a relationship with an employee. In other words, leadership is fundamentally based on human interaction.

> **" COMMUNICATION IS NOT SIMPLY A MEDIUM THROUGH WHICH LEADERSHIP HAPPENS TO BE EXERCISED; IT IS PART OF ITS SUBSTANCE . . . LEADERSHIP IS FUNDAMENTALLY BASED ON HUMAN INTERACTION. "**

Proposition 2: Leadership is fundamentally dialogical

Dialogue has been applied to organizational and leadership communication settings, e.g., in discussion about its ethics and legitimacy (Heath et al., 2006), dialogue's linguistics (Barge & Little, 2002), and cognitive dialogue theory (Cohen, 2004). In this study, dialogue is seen as an interpersonal relationship. The view is based on the conceptualization proposed by Buber (1957/2006).

Buber (1957/2006, pp. 7–8) describes the interpersonal nature of human existence through two concepts constituted by two pairs of words, dialogue (I–Thou) and monologue (I–It). The pairs of words categorize the dual modes of consciousness and interaction through which a human being engages with other human beings. In dialogue the two terms, I and Thou, encounter each other in a relationship. In this mutual exchange I becomes Thou (subject–subject). In other words, the I and Thou relationship is a direct, reciprocal interpersonal relationship where human beings are aware of each other as having a unity of being (Buber, 1957/2006, pp. 19, 32–34).

In a monologue relationship between I and It, I confronts an idea of the being in its presence. In other words, It is treated as an object (subject–object) (Buber, 1957/ 2006, p. 27). Thus, the relationship and hence interaction occurs in the mental representations of the individual mind and only becomes actual first when it changes into an I–Thou relationship (Buber, 1957/2006, pp. 16–17, 37). For human beings mental representations are endogenous. However, as Buber (1957/2006, p. 38) states, a person who lives only in a reality of I and It and treats others as objects is not a human being. So long as we are engaged in communication with others, we are engaged in a dialogical process that continually shapes and reshapes ourselves and others, and our relationship to each other. In other words, all reality and communication is laden with the traces of other people with whom we interact (Barge & Little, 2002, pp. 378–395).

As stated earlier, leadership occurs in a relationship. Consequently, reciprocal relationships between leaders and employees are based on dialogue. When a leader engages in a relationship with an employee, the relationship becomes mutual: the It becomes Thou (see Buber, 1957/2006, p. 37). Thus, the relationship between a leader and an employee is a two-way relationship where both parties acknowledge each other's contribution to the interaction. Dialogue represents and emphasizes notions of equality, otherness, and freedom in human interaction (Spitzberg & Cupach, 2002, p. 582).

Proposition 3: Dialogue is part of leadership communication competence

As leadership occurs in a relationship, a communicatively competent leader has the same ability to engage in a relationship as he or she has in dialogue. Leadership communication competence can be defined through the concept of interpersonal communication competence. As Spitzberg and Cupach (1984) propose, interpersonal communication competence can be seen as consisting of three elements: *knowledge, skills,* and *motivation.* The latest research adds two more elements to the definition: *meta-cognitive skills* and *ethical principles.* The value given to specific communication competencies is dependent on how *appropriate* and *effective* communication behaviour is perceived to be in accomplishing the goals of the particular communication relationship or situation (see, for example, Spitzberg & Dillard, 2002; Valkonen, 2003; Wilson & Sabee, 2003).

Thus, leadership communication competence includes the cognitive competencies, knowledge and skills, that help leaders to orchestrate dialogue and to adapt their individual actions to the intentions of others, develop shared intentions, and thereby participate and lead collective action (Cohen, 2004, pp. 178–179). Moreover, leadership communication competence includes the meta-cognitive skills needed to form a judgment about an effective and appropriate way of entering into an interpersonal relationship and to identify the attitudes with which the participants in the interaction approach each other, the ways they talk and interact, the consequences of their meetings, and the context within which they meet. In other words, leadership communication competence includes meta-cognitive abilities to engage in dialogue (see Cissna & Anderson, 1998, p. 64).

At the very least, as dialogue is a special way of thinking about and taking a stand together with another participant in a communication situation, dialogue is also connected to the ethical principles of leadership communication competence (see Barge & Little, 2002, pp. 367–377). The ethical dimensions of dialogue as a leadership communication competence include not hurting the other party in an interpersonal relationship, and not putting the relationship at risk (see Valkonen, 2003, p. 26).

Wilson and Sabee (2003, p. 32) suggest that the qualities needed for communication competence should be re-envisioned as qualities of a relationship at a particular place and time rather than qualities of individual communicators. However, insight into interpersonal communication competence in a leadership setting and dialogue as part of it can be achieved through investigating the leader's work tasks and the communication behaviour in them or how these are perceived by the participants of the given interpersonal relationship.

Study Framework and Research Questions

The purpose of the study is to investigate the three theoretical propositions presented above and to find out *what kind of interpersonal communication competence is essential for leaders in a knowledge-based organization.* To do this requires finding out how leadership communication and leadership communication competence are perceived in a knowledge-based organization, whether leadership communication in such an organization really is dialogical, and whether a dialogical way of thinking can be connected with the concept of leadership communication competence. Two research questions are addressed:

> RQ1: How do leaders working in a knowledge-based organization perceive communication and interpersonal communication competence as a part of leadership?

> RQ2: How do leaders working in a knowledge-based organization perceive dialogue as a part of leadership communication and leadership communication competence?

Method
Procedure and Participants

This study forms part of a doctoral dissertation concerning the interpersonal communication competence of leaders and the effectiveness of training and developing such competence in a knowledge-based organization. The study is a case study and concentrates on a leadership development program carried out in a Finnish knowledge-based organization with 300 employees. The leaders and key personnel of the organization took a Special Degree in Leadership (Johtamisen erikoisammattitutkinto, JET) during the years 2005–2007.

The organization in question is a research and development organization. Its organizational activities include research, development, and customer services. The organization is divided into three different units: the research and development unit is organized as a process-based matrix organization where customer projects are carried out ad hoc at different organizational levels between different competence areas and teams, the customer service unit is organized as a hierarchical line organization, and the administrative headquarters is organized in teams according to the administrative task in question.

The results presented in this paper are based on interviews with leadership personnel ($N = 17$) taking the Special Degree in Leadership. The leadership personnel who were interviewed work in various management and leadership positions in the organization. The participants in this study each lead between four and thirty administrative staff. Ten of the leaders are women, seven are men. Their working experience in management and leadership ranges from six months to over twenty years, and all have worked for the target organization for between less than one year and more than ten years. The interviews were conducted before the beginning of the leadership development program. The interviews were thematic in nature and lasted on average for one hour.

Analysis

The data gathered from the interviews were analyzed qualitatively using the constant comparative model by Strauss and Corbin (1990) and the cross-case approach by Miles and Huberman (1994). In the constant comparative model interpretation rested on teasing out, discovering, formulating, and naming categories; making comparisons; and the evolving putting-togetherness of the theoretical framework (Strauss & Corbin, 1990). The inspection and comparison of data fragments were done first within a single case (Silverman, 2005, p. 214). In the cross-case analysis, in turn, the focus was first on each case (a single interview) and afterwards on the comparison of different cases (seventeen interviews) (Huberman & Miles, 1994, pp. 435–437).

Before the data were analyzed, the interviews were transcribed. For organizing and managing the data, the ATLAS.ti program was used. The inductive analysis of the actual data proceeded gradually. First the data were coded openly. The open coding included labeling the phenomena and teasing out categories by putting different questions to the data. This coding step aimed to elaborate the categories in terms of their properties and dimensions. The open coding procedure identified twenty-two different categories of perceptions connected to leadership communication competence in a knowledge-based organization.

Secondly, the data were coded axially and displayed in matrices and tables. The categories were compared and connections between the categories were sought. Axial coding produced the following six categories: meanings given to leadership tasks, leadership communication, leadership communication competence, leadership communication challenges in a knowledge-based organization, and one's own leadership communication competence and the need to develop it.

Thirdly, conclusions were drawn by noting underlying similarities and differences as well as systematic associations between cases. Thus, the selective coding procedure identified the core category of valued leadership communication that integrated the previous levels of the analysis and through which the different communication characteristics and challenges of leadership in a knowledge-based organization can be screened. The findings are presented in the next section.

Findings

Generally, the leaders interviewed perceived communication to play an important role in leadership. In most cases leadership communication competence was defined through the different communicational challenges presented by purposive work. First of all, in a knowledge-based organization social capital was experienced as individualized across the organization. In addition, an uncertain and dynamic working environment was seen to lead to insecurity. A sense of insecurity, in turn, was seen to lead to competition for both posts and work to do, and workmates were seen as competitors rather than colleagues. When addressing working atmosphere in the interview situation, one of the leaders defined his or her task the following way:

> All together, you have to create a positive atmosphere so that people are open and trust each other and then, that it is nice to be at work. So that the atmosphere can be positive. (Leader 1)[†]

The leader quoted defined the leader's task as creating a positive working atmosphere in order to support trust between employees. Altogether, the leaders reported that because of the competition for things to do, knowledge was not easily shared but was kept by the individual to him/herself. Consequently, the leaders saw it as their task to network inside the organization; to bring human resources together in projects; and to create an open, trusting, and inspiring working atmosphere at meetings.

Motivating employees and supporting collaborative communication and work were perceived as challenging. In discussion about teamwork, one leader emphasized the challenges facing leadership communication when seeking to support collaborative work:

[†]The Finnish excerpts were translated into English by the author.

Usually when you have a project team that is working well, everybody is active, everybody is discussing, people disagree, people are able to interact, and everybody is doing something. . . . I often don't see it. I go to the meetings and I see big teams of people and many of them are being silent and not contributing and you have the feeling that people don't care in a way. So, I don't really see the skills in a lot of the project managers to actually lead that team. They can do the mechanical management, but not the leadership part. (Leader 15)

The excerpt above illustrates the opinion that a good teamwork situation is characterized by participation, discussion, and also disagreement. Leadership is conceptualized as leading team members to contribute actively, and to discuss and disagree. Moreover, the speaker emphasizes the importance of leadership communication skills in supporting collaborative group interaction. However, the leader quoted reported a lack of leadership skills in this area in the organization.

Expertise and purposive work was perceived on the personal level and thus giving feedback and guidance was challenging. These were conceptualized as performed best by listening and asking as the work area might not have been within the domain of expertise of the leader. In addition, leadership communication was reported to be especially important when leaders are working and communicating with critical-thinking, highly educated subordinates:

Having a researcher's education leads to deep criticism, questioning everything. That is an interesting characteristic and presents its own challenge to the leadership. (Leader 10)

The quotation shows how a researcher's education, which many of the employees have, was seen to lead to deep criticism and questioning of organizational decisions. In consequence, critically minded subordinates were mentioned as demanding involvement. For example, according to the leaders' opinions, critical-thinking subordinates should be included to some extent in such leadership processes as strategy and decision making:

When strategies are being worked out there is a lot of planning to do. And you can't do very much of that alone. It is a kind of communication, communication in both directions. (Leader 5)

The leader quoted states that it is essential to involve employees in the strategy process because of the amount of planning involved. He or she conceptualizes communication as communicating in both directions, upward and downward. In addition, the leaders interviewed in the research and development unit did not want to lead by giving orders but by guiding and facilitating.

However, the relationship with employees and the communication with them were conceptualized in various ways. Although the leaders of the research unit valued the expertise of their employees, not all perceived communicating as empowering and involving. According to one leader, in contrast to the researchers demanding involvement, some of the employees in the service unit expected clear guidance:

> I feel that in [the name of the organization] the workers wait for the opinion and acceptance of the manager or leader. Sometimes it works only when [the name of the CEO] or I say things aloud. It is quite funny. It is as if people feel that only the top leadership has the whole mandate, responsibility, and authority. (Leader 16)

As the extract above shows, the communication culture of the service unit was seen as wanting hierarchical decision making and guidance. The leader reported that only the communication of the top leadership was believed and trusted.

Some of the leaders in the service unit considered it essential for a leader to take actions, assign tasks, and talk in a simple and down-to-earth manner. The leaders in the service unit wanted to encourage their employees to participate in organizational discussion. However, they found this challenging because of the lack of interest on the part of the employees. Consequently, planning and decision making was seen in some of the teams as best carried out alone without employee input. This, however, was seen by one of the leaders as a delicate process:

> The supervisor cannot tell the employees everything, but the supervisor needs to know what kind of information could be beneficial and what it is that an employee needs to know. (Leader 11)

The leader's role was seen as informing and communicating the decisions of the top leadership to those further down the hierarchy. The leader quoted below sees his or her task as one of deciding what information is useful for the employees to know, what information to pass on, and what information to withhold.

For some of the leaders, the relationship with employees was seen as a superior-subordinate relationship, for others employees were more like equal colleagues. The following extract exemplifies the latter attitude despite the existence of formal organizational structures that define managerial positions:

I think in this kind of researcher community where you are in a research area management position you are not a better expert. Everyone is an expert in their own area from where the creative work comes and from whom the ideas come. It is always cooperation. These are very smart people, probably a lot smarter than I am. I am not under that kind of illusion. I just have this role and this task [manager]. (Leader 17)

According to this account, creative work is based on cooperation between experts from different areas of expertise where the leader is not necessarily a better expert.

In most cases expert work was conceptualized as cooperation where the leader's role was to point to the organizational goal and give the employees enough space to execute their assignments and express their opinions. Consequently, according to the leaders interviewed, leadership communication includes listening and taking several opinions into consideration. Some leaders even described their work and the human interaction in it by direct reference to the concept of dialogue:

It is clear that they expect me to say something and they listen to me. Partly it is a kind of dialogue that I have to know, since they know the thing and the project better, how to ask what they suggest that we should do, etc. (Leader 1)

The extract above illustrates one leader's conceptualization of dialogue. This leader defines him/herself on the one hand as a superior who is listened to. On the other hand he or she has to know how to ask the employees for their opinion and to work in a dialogical way in order to bring out their expertise.

Looking at the seventeen interviews, it can be said that the leaders' perceptions about leadership communication and whether it should be involving and empowering or instructing and guiding varied widely. The findings are discussed in more detail in the next section.

Discussion

The goal of this study was to examine what kind of interpersonal communication competence is essential for leaders in a knowledge-based organization; that is, how leaders themselves perceive interpersonal communication competence as a part of leadership, and how they perceive dialogue as a part of leadership communication competence. In order to do so, an approach combining the concepts of dialogue and leadership communication competence was applied, with the focus on the opinions and experiences of leadership personnel about their work and the human interaction situations it involves.

According to the opinions and experiences of the leaders, human interaction and communication play a significant role in leadership. Leadership was defined through collaborative and communicational practices and even through dialogue. Thus, Proposition 1, "Leadership is fundamentally based on human interaction," was partly supported.

The opinions and experiences of leaders about their work support earlier studies on the challenges of leading in a knowledge-based organization. In a knowledge-based organization, the management of knowledge and organizational networks—in other words, social interaction between human beings—is central to efficiency and success (e.g., Heaton & Taylor, 2002; Huotari, Hurme, & Valkonen, 2005). The findings of this study indicate that, according to the leaders, leaders play a key role in helping an organization's members to cope with the challenges arising out of a dynamic environment. Leadership communication seems to be of central importance in bringing the expertise of the organization together, and facilitating and securing a collaborative culture of interaction.

The results of this study also partly support the features of a human resource organization where the organization's members are not only consulted when management and leaders make decisions, but also encouraged to actively participate in making decisions that affect their tasks and the organization (Jablin & Sias, 2001, pp. 845–846). The potential of critical-thinking employees and involvement of various voices in decision making were partly acknowledged in the organization studied here. According to the opinions and experiences of the leaders, as purposive work is perceived as personal and thus largely independent as opposed to assigned work, it cannot be guided by telling alone and without listening. Thus, according to the leaders, leadership dialogue means taking account of the various voices of the organization. Purposive work and its personalized character counterpoint the importance of equality and otherness in leadership relationships and consequently the communicational nature of leadership and the interconnectedness of leadership communication competence and dialogue.

However, leaders' perceptions of leadership communication varied from the hierarchical supervisor-subordinate type of relationship to the collegial relationship, and from monologue to dialogue. The leaders' conceptualizations of dialogue seem to subscribe to the view that leadership communication is in many aspects information dissemination, and that the supervisor is still in some aspects superior to those in his charge. In addition, collaborative and collective work as well as leadership communication were in some cases conceptualized as leader-led. Thus, the leaders' perceptions question the assumption about the dialogical nature of leadership. In this respect it can be said that leadership communication was not always seen as dialogical in nature even if dialogue was seen as a valued way to communicate and lead. In sum, Proposition 2, "Leadership is fundamentally dialogical," was not entirely supported. Consequently, Proposition 3, "Dialogue is part of leadership communication competence," was not entirely supported either.

 LEADERSHIP COMMUNICATION SEEMS TO BE OF CENTRAL IMPORTANCE IN BRINGING THE EXPERTISE OF THE ORGANIZATION TOGETHER, AND FACILITATING AND SECURING A COLLABORATIVE CULTURE OF INTERACTION.

Although the theoretical assumptions were not supported by all of the leaders interviewed, this study provides a new insight into leadership communication as well as leadership communication competence in contemporary organizations. The results contribute to the existing research on leadership communication competence in knowledge-based organizations in the following ways: competent leadership communication is essential in networking, managing knowledge, motivating and inspiring employees, supporting collaborative work, facilitating group discussions and problem-solving, involving employees in decision making and the strategy process, listening, and giving feedback and consulting in expertise and purposive work. Interpersonally competent leadership communication in a knowledge-based organization seems to be both open, caring, and sensitive as well as determined and assertive.

The problem of combining leadership communication competence and dialogue is that leadership is traditionally conceptualized as goal-oriented and leader-led action. In general, power relations are seen as limiting dialogue (Heath et al., 2006, p. 370). Yet, leadership and dialogue are not contradictory concepts. From the viewpoint of dialogue, guidance in knowledge-intensive and purposive work is not giving orders but negotiating about the meaning of the work and its accomplishment. A dialogue-based view of leadership includes the assumption that the leader is not superior in organizational communication even if his or her role is to communicate in a goal-oriented way and to persuade. Competent leadership communication includes taking multiple goals into consideration. In addition, dialogical communication is always on the border between that which we can control and that which we cannot, and it is a process that shapes us as much as we shape it (Heath et al., 2006, pp. 345–346).

Limitations

To find out about the interpersonal communication competence perceptions of leaders in a knowledge-based organization, the focus was on the opinions and experiences of leadership personnel about their work and human interaction in it. This was done with a set of conceptually specified analytical categories and step-by-step analysis. As a result, this study provided a comparative insight into a typical contemporary organization and in this way produced new knowledge in the area of leadership communication and interpersonal communication competence. However, as a case study, one should be cautious about generalizing the findings to other contexts. Instead, one could evaluate the results through the criteria of transferability to another situation (see Guba & Lincoln, 1985).

The analytical method used in this study made a systematic comparison of cases possible, even though the amount of data was small (Huberman & Miles, 1994, p. 436). However, the analysis of the data can be deepened further (e.g., by comparing factors that are present in every case, those that are present in some cases and not others, and those that are entirely absent). Furthermore, when studying leadership communication competence from an interpersonal point of view it is essential also to canvass the perceptions of employees. This appoints a new research task for investigating leadership dialogue and interpersonal communication competence.

Conclusions

The results of this study indicate that leadership communication competence is an area that merits more research attention in relation to contemporary knowledge-based organizations and purposive work. There is a need for a more philosophical approach to the underpinnings of leadership and leadership communication. For this purpose dialogue and interpersonal communication competence are multidimensional and feasible concepts.

 DIALOGUE IS THE KEY FACTOR FOR COLLABORATIVE WORK AND INTERACTION IN ORGANIZATIONS. ❞❞

A dialogical and interpersonal communication competence-based perspective on leadership communication research also has many possible practical implications. For example, an interpersonal communication competence-based conception of dialogue can provide a better understanding of complex communicative and interactive practices of organizations and provide guidance for its practitioners and developers. Perhaps the most important aspect of dialogue is its potential to inspire the unique and the creative processes of human interaction (see Heath et al., 2006, pp. 354, 369). Communicational practices that encourage employee involvement provide a more complex environment for interaction, and organizational members and leaders can engage in a dialogical way also in traditionally non-dialogic practices such as decision making and strategy planning and implementation (Zorn & Violanti, 1996, p. 161). Dialogue is the key factor for collaborative work and interaction in organizations. Leaders, in turn, are in the key position in the organization to embolden and reinforce it with their communicatively competent behavior.

Acknowledgments

This paper is based on the author's doctoral dissertation, currently in preparation and supervised by Professor Tarja Valkonen, PhD, Department of Communication, University of Jyväskylä (Finland). The research focuses on the interpersonal communication competence of leaders and how it can effectively be developed in a knowledge-based organization. The author wishes to thank the anonymous reviewers and the editors of Building Leadership Bridges for their valuable comments. The research has been supported by grants from the Alfred Kordelin Foundation, Emil Aaltonen Foundation, Finnish Cultural Foundation, Finnish Work Environment Fund, and the University of Jyväskylä.

REFERENCES

Barge, J. K. (1994). *Leadership: Communication skills for organizations and groups*. New York: St. Martin's.

Barge, J. K., & Little, M. (2002). Dialogical wisdom, communicative practice, and organizational life. *Communication Theory, 12*, 375–397.

Buber, M. (2006). Ich und Du. In M. Buber, *Das Dialogische Prinzip* (10th ed., pp. 7–136). München: Gütersloher Verlagshaus. (Original work published 1957)

Cissna, K. N., & Anderson, R. (1998). Theorizing about dialogical moments: The Buber-Rogers position and postmodern themes. *Communication Theory, 8*, 63–104.

Cohen, M. S. (2004). Leadership as the orchestration and improvisation of dialogue: Cognitive and communicative skills in conversations among leaders and subordinates. In D. V. Day, S. J. Zaccaro, & S. M. Halpin (Eds.), *Leader development for transforming organizations: Growing leaders for tomorrow* (pp. 177–208). Mahwah, NJ: Lawrence Erlbaum Associates.

Fairhurst, G. T. (2001). Dualism in leadership research. In F. M. Jablin & L. L. Putnam (Eds.), *The new handbook of organizational communication: Advances in theory, research, and methods* (pp. 379–439). Thousand Oaks, CA: Sage Publications.

Flanagin, A. J., Stohl, C., & Bimber, B. (2006). Modeling the structure of collective action. *Communication Monographs, 73*, 29–54.

Flauto, F. J. (1999). Walking the talk: The relationship between leadership and communication competence. *The Journal of Leadership Studies, 6*, 86–96.

Guba, E. G., & Lincoln, Y. S. (1985). *Naturalistic inquiry*. Beverly Hills, CA: Sage Publications.

Hackman, M. Z., & Johnson, C. E. (2004). *Leadership: A communication perspective* (4th ed). Prospect Heights, IL: Waveland Press.

Heath, R. L., Pearce, W. B., Shotter, J., Taylor, J. R., Kersten, A., Zorn, T., Roper, J., Motion, J., & Deetz, S. (2006). The processes of dialogue: Participation and legitimation. *Management Communication Quarterly, 19*, 341–375.

Heaton, L., & Taylor, J. R. (2002). Knowledge management and professional work: A communication perspective on the knowledge-based organization. *Management Communication Quarterly, 16,* 210–236.

Huberman, A. M., & Miles, M. B. (1994). Data management and analysis methods. In N. K. Denzin & Y. S. Lincoln (Eds.), *Handbook of qualitative research* (pp. 428–444). Thousand Oaks, CA: Sage Publications.

Huotari, M.-L., Hurme, P., & Valkonen, T. (2005). Viestinnästä tietoon. Tiedon luominen työyhteisössä [*From communication to knowledge. Interaction and knowledge creation in organizations*]. Helsinki, Finland: WSOY.

Jablin, F. M., & Sias, P. M. (2001). Communication competence. In F. M. Jablin & L. L. Putnam (Eds.), *The new handbook of organizational communication: Advances in theory, research, and methods* (pp. 819–864). Thousand Oaks, CA: Sage Publications.

Miles, M., & Huberman, A. M. (1994). *Qualitative data analysis: An expanded sourcebook* (2nd ed.). Thousand Oaks, CA: Sage Publications.

Silverman, D. (2005). *Doing qualitative research* (2nd ed.). London: Sage Publications.

Spitzberg, B. H., & Cupach, W. R. (1984). *Interpersonal communication competence.* Beverly Hills, CA: Sage Publications.

Spitzberg, B. H., & Cupach, W. R. (2002). Interpersonal skills. In M. L. Knapp & J. A. Daly (Eds.), *Handbook of interpersonal communication* (3rd ed., pp. 564–611). Thousand Oaks, CA: Sage Publications.

Spitzberg, B. H., & Dillard, J. P. (2002). Social skills and communication. In M. Allen, R. W. Preiss, B. M. Gayle, & N. A. Burrel (Eds.), *Interpersonal communication research. Advances through meta-analysis* (pp. 89–107). Mahwah, NJ: Lawrence Erlbaum Associates.

Strauss, A. L., & Corbin, J. (1998). *Basics of qualitative research: Grounded theory procedures and techniques* (2nd ed.). Newbury Park, CA: Sage Publications.

Taylor, J. R., Flanagin, A.J., Cheney, G., & Seibold, D. R. (2000). Organizational communication research: Key moments, central concerns, and future challenges. In W. B. Gudykunst (Ed.), *Communication Yearbook, 24,* 99–137. Thousand Oaks, CA: Sage Publications.

Tourish, D., & Hargie, O. (1999). Communication and organizational success. In O. Hargie, D. Dickson, & D. Tourish (Eds.), *Communication in management* (pp. 3–21). Aldershot, UK: Gower.

Valkonen, T. (2003). Puheviestintätaitojen arviointi: Näkökulmia lukiolaisten esiintymis-ja ryhmätaitoihin [*Assessing speech communication skills: Perspectives on presentation and group communication skills among upper secondary school students*]. Studies in Humanities 7. University of Jyväskylä.

Wilson, S. R., & Sabee, C. M. (2003). Explicating communication competence as a theoretical term. In J. O. Greene & B. R. Burleson (Eds.), *Handbook of communication and social interaction skills* (pp. 3–50). Mahwah, NJ: Lawrence Erlbaum Associates.

Zorn, T. E., & Violanti, M. T. (1996). Communication abilities and individual achievement in organizations. *Management Communication Quarterly, 10,* 139–167.

MAIJASTIINA ROUHIAINEN, MA, is a doctoral student in speech communication at the University of Jyväskylä, Finland. Her doctoral dissertation explores the interpersonal communication competence of leaders and how it can be effectively developed in a knowledge-based organization.

Do Transformational Leaders Speak Differently?

The Impact of Leaders' Transformational Communications in Meeting Followers' Implicit Leadership Prototypes

By Charles Salter, Meghan Carmody-Bubb, Phyllis Duncan, and Mark T. Green

OVER THE YEARS LEADERSHIP HAS BEEN STUDIED FROM A NUMBER of approaches. Trait theories were a first attempt to look into what characteristics a person should have to become an effective leader (Mann, 1959; Stogdill, 1948). Researchers soon recognized that one of the deficiencies of trait theory was its adoption of the leader as a homogeneous role player, autonomous to the variations in the leader-follower dynamic across differing environments. Hollander and Julian (1969) suggested that the increased interest in the situational aspects of leadership resulted from recognition that there were specific situational demands made on leaders, depending upon the task of the group and other situational variables. Researchers' recognition of the inability of trait analysis to fully explain leadership utility initially led to the behavioral style approach, which suggested situational variables moderate a leader's effectiveness (Fiedler, 1967; Hersey & Blanchard, 1969).

French and Raven (1959), in their research on social power, asserted that a leader may influence a follower using different bases of power. The researchers further stated that an ability to influence a follower is accorded to the leader by the follower, and without follower acceptability, a legitimate leader's power to influence is hindered. Barbuto, Fritz, and Matkin (2001) suggest that French and Raven's (1959) bases of social power are related to transformational and transactional leadership.

Recognizing follower acceptance as a key element in leadership effectiveness has led researchers to investigate followers as a primary environmental link to organizational success. The need to understand followers as a situational variable and their relationship to the leader's effectiveness has influenced research in follower traits (Felfe & Schyns, 2006; Salter, Green, & Ree, 2006), cognitive processes and perception, attribution theory, and implied values and behaviors a follower identifies with effective leadership (Calder, 1977; Lord, 1985; Lord, DeVader, & Alliger, 1986; Lord & Maher, 1990).

Cognition, Communication, and Implicit Leadership

Graen and Cashman (1975) suggest dyadic relationships between leaders and followers and, more importantly, the perceptions and expectations of those relationships by the follower are critical determinants of a follower's willingness to be influenced by the leader (Lord, 1977).

Calder (1977) suggests that role schemas or a set of normative expectations help followers in their understanding and interpretation of observed leader behaviors. The researcher further states that the term *leadership* is the language given to behaviors which are consistent with the observer's leadership schemas. Phillips and Lord (1981) indicate that a follower's perception of a leadership behavior by a stimulus creates a leader category, where the behavior is compared to the observer's schema of the behaviors of their prototypical leader.

Research investigating implicit leadership theories (Lord, Foti, & DeVader, 1984) found that individuals use categories of behavior to define leader and non-leader behavior, as well as to assess effective versus ineffective leadership behavior. These categories largely consist of communication types of behaviors, and the authors further suggest that the perceiver's characterizing others into personality categories involves matching the perceived behavior of the leader into perceiver prototypes.

Cognitive Processes and Prediction of Leader Behavior

Concerning cognitive processes, Mischel (1977) argued that traits and behaviors of leaders are important constructs for perceivers. These constructs aid them in organizing perceptions of others into memory categories or schemas. Mischel goes on to say that individuals seem to have an innate security need which is satisfied by prototyping a leader and placing these expectations of behavior in memory categories. Eden and Leviathan (1975) further suggest communication and trust of a leader are enhanced when followers have prototyped a leader's traits so accurately that they can predict the leader's behavior in particular situations. These authors also purported that a leader's behaviors guide a perceiver's encoding of relevant information, which is then utilized by the perceiver to aid in decision making concerning tasks associated with the leader. Moreover, evidence from Lord and Maher (1991) suggests that this process aids in memory, as they found that a follower's recall of leadership informational instructions was enhanced if the follower had correctly prototyped the traits and behaviors of the leader. Furthermore, Winter and Uleman (1984) indicated that this process of making trait inferences when encoding into memory takes place unconsciously. Such evidence suggests an innate universal need on the part of the perceiver to encode into memory a leader's traits or behaviors as categorizations of predictability. This has led researchers to look for a universal list of traits or behaviors recognizable to followers that would precipitate followers' categorizations of predictability of a leader.

Hollander and Julian (1969) suggest a number of expectations a follower would have of an effective leader. An effective leader should: (1) be a resource of adequate role behavior directed toward meeting the goals of the group, (2) initiate structure by setting goals and priorities, (3) function as a mediator of group disturbances, (4) be the group spokesperson outside the group, (5) provide rewards, (6) be competent in helping the group meet its goals, (7) facilitate motivation regarding the attainment of the group goals, (8) show a personal interest in group members, (9) show signs of identification with the group, and (10) initiate a participative form of decision making which invokes critical thinking for mutual goal attainment.

The Full Range Leadership Model and Follower Expectations

The discussion above indicates that Implicit Leadership Theories are connected with a follower's preconception or prototype of an effective leader's behaviors. As researchers have found, those connections consist, in part, of dyadic interactions with followers. Pursuing Hollander and Julian's (1969) aforementioned list of followers' behavioral expectations of effective leaders, one can readily match these expectations

 IMPLICIT LEADERSHIP THEORIES ARE CONNECTED WITH A FOLLOWER'S PRECONCEPTION OR PROTOTYPE OF AN EFFECTIVE LEADER'S BEHAVIORS. **"**

to Bass and Avolio's (1994) Full Range Leadership Model of transactional and transformational leadership. Hollander and Julian's (1969) follower expectations of an effective leader as a role model, as an inspirational motivator, as one showing individualized concern for followers, and as a participative leader invoking critical thinking are very consistent with Bass and Avolio's (1994) description of a transformational leader who demonstrates idealized influence or charisma, individualized consideration, being an inspirational motivator, and providing intellectual stimulation through participative forms of leadership.

Given Hollander and Julian's (1969) list of follower expectations of effective leaders' behaviors, and the similar description of the charismatic component of transformational leadership (Bass & Avolio, 1994) described by House (1976), as well as Graen and Cashman's (1975) suggestions that the expectations of followers are at least in part influenced by dyadic relationships with leaders, have led to research centered around leader/follower interrelationships and the communications of the effective leader.

Transformational Leadership, Implicit Leadership, and Interpersonal Communication

Investigating transformational leadership as a dyadic relationship or a set of communications between the leader and followers' implicit expectations suggests that a leader's behavior is evident in his or her communication to followers. In particular, effective leaders speak to followers in ways that build unity of purpose and increased bridges for shared visions and culture.

Hackman and Johnson (2000) suggest leadership may best be understood from a communication perspective, and go on to describe leadership as a human symbolic communication which modifies the attitudes and behaviors of others in an attempt to meet shared group goals. Johnson, Vinson, Hackman, and Hardin (1989) state that an individual's willingness to communicate is a necessary ingredient in one emerging as a leader in group settings. Clutterback and Hirst (2002) and Caroselli (2005) found that an effective transformational leader must be an effective communicator, a purveyor of meaning who uses analogy and metaphor to elucidate in the follower a vivid image of some future ideal state. Related research on communication and transformational leadership (Burleson, 1987; Flauto, 1999) has indicated that a leader with a well-developed system of interpersonal communication can understand listeners in a complex and abstract psychological framework, allowing the communicator to develop messages of particular interest to the listener.

Transformational Language

Burleson (1987) referred to these communicators/leaders as *highly differentiated communicators.* Sypher (1981) found that highly differentiated individuals were considered by their superiors to be more effective. Furthermore, Sypher and Zorn (1986) found that those who used more person-centered communication advanced to higher positions in their organizations than those who were not highly differentiated communicators. Zorn (1991) established that individuals who rated highly as transformational leaders also had high scores on the attributes associated with highly differentiated communicators. Further research on communication and leadership emergence and effectiveness has led researchers to sequester leader emergence into categories associated with shorter and longer social interactions. Riggio, Riggio, Salinas, and Cole (2003) found that in groups of shorter interaction time, leader emergence was defined by the amount of words an individual spoke, or what Bass (1990) referred to as the babble hypothesis. However, these same authors noted in an additional sample that in social situations requiring longer periods of time and more in-depth problem-solving, the quality of the communication affected leader emergence.

" EFFECTIVE LEADERS SPEAK TO FOLLOWERS IN WAYS THAT BUILD UNITY OF PURPOSE AND INCREASED BRIDGES FOR SHARED VISIONS AND CULTURE. "

The above research motivates one to consider transformational leaders as highly differentiated communicators who meet the implicit expectations of followers with their communications. DeSteno, Petty, Rucker, Wegener, and Braverman (2004) suggest that persuasion is more manifest and effective when garnered within the bounds of emotional communications. Additionally, Kennedy (1994) emphasizes the importance of emotional communications by quoting Marcus Tullius Cicero as saying, "... for everyone knows that the power of the orator is most manifest in dealing with people's feelings, when he is stirring them to anger or to hatred and resentment, or is calling them back from these same emotions to mildness and compassion" (p. 106). Bass (1990) states that transformational leaders stimulate the higher mental processes of their followers through the use of symbolic, emotional language and in so doing satisfies a need in the follower.

While direct studies of the language used by leaders are limited, Bligh, Kohles, and Meindl (2004) cite a number of researchers (Conger, 1991; Insch, Moore, & Murphey, 1997; Thayer, 1988) as supporting the idea that "the leadership relationship is fundamentally rooted in language and communication" (p. 563). The authors stress that there is a need for "research that more explicitly addresses the symbolic, linguistic, and contextual elements surrounding and embedding the leadership process (p. 562). In their own study entitled *Charting the Language of Leadership: A Methodological Investigation of President Bush and the Crisis of 9/11*, Bligh et al. (2004) conducted a content analysis of the speeches of the president pre- and post-9/11, as well as the language conveyed by the media. Citing several researchers (Bass, 1990; Bunker, 1986; George, 2000; Kelloway & Barling, 2000), they suggested "a number of characteristics that might become more prevalent in a postcrisis environment, including optimism, bold and directive leadership, and collective support" (p. 563).

Bligh et al. (2004) specifically related these characteristics to transformational leadership, citing several authors whose research suggests "the ability of leaders to raise the salience of collective identities is a critical element of transformational leadership" (p. 563). As such, the authors reasoned that the rhetoric in both the presidential speeches and the media reporting on those speeches would contain "more references to the American people and the patriotic and Judeo-Christian themes that have historically united them" (p. 563). The authors examined six constructs for differences in rhetoric pre- and post-9/11. Results indicated significant differences for five of the constructs (collectives, faith, patriotism, aggression, and ambivalence), indicating that "in the wake of the crisis of 9/11, President Bush's speeches were more likely to reference the American people as a collective and incorporate more patriotic, faith-based themes . . . [and to be] more aggressive and less ambivalent" (p. 565). No significant differences between pre- and post-9/11 rhetoric were found for the construct, optimism. The authors repeated the analysis for a sample of media coverage, with similar findings.

An Empirical Study of Language Use

To further expand the base of knowledge regarding leadership and communication as established by the previous research discussed above, the current study investigated the relationship between the leader's transformational and effectiveness ratings and the leader's usage of particular word units in a work setting.

Twenty-five executives from an international construction company were selected by the Chief Executive Officer for a three-week intensive leadership development program at Our Lady of the Lake University. The participants were predominantly white males. The majority of participants held bachelor's degrees and had been in leadership positions for at least ten years.

Instruments

As part of the training program, participants submitted a 360-degree evaluation. Each participant's leader, two coworkers, and three followers completed the following instruments on each leader: the MLQ Form 5X and the Job Descriptor Index (JDI). The initial and cross-validation study of the MLQ Form 5X was used to test the convergent and discriminate validities of each scale through confirmatory factor analysis. The studies consisted of examining nine samples with a total $N = 2,154$, and a second study using five samples with a total $N = 1,706$; these two studies combined for a total of 14 samples and a total of $N = 3,860$. Reliabilities for the total items and leadership factor scales ranged from .74 to .94. The validity coefficient for the MLQ is .91 (Bass & Avolio, 2000).

The abridged version of the Job in General (JIG) was designed to offer the advantages of a very brief instrument without sacrificing the psychometric properties of the full-length version of the JIG (Russell, Spitzmuller, Stanton, Smith, & Ironson, 2004). Stanton (2000) developed a visual basic software program that compiles all possible combinations of a user-defined number of items, sorted by magnitude of correlation with a full-length scale score. The resulting list can then be analyzed for preferences for phrasing of words, or balancing positively and negatively worded items. The distributions of correlations produced by this technique require cross-validation techniques with additional samples. Russell et al. (2004) used three studies to carefully develop and cross-validate an abridged version of the JIG (AJIG) scale by following recommendations and procedures from Stanton (2000) and Stanton, Sinar, Blazer, and Smith (2002). The final set of eight adjectives making up the AJIG yielded an alpha coefficient of .87 and correlated strongly with the original scale, $r = .97$ (Russell et al., 2004).

The abridged version of the JDI (AJDI) consists of twenty five items and measures five aspects of employee satisfaction: satisfaction with work, satisfaction with pay, satisfaction with opportunities for promotion, satisfaction with supervision, and satisfaction with coworkers. Both the AJIG and AJDI were used in the 360-degree evaluations. To further understand how these participants actually engaged in transformational leadership, participants answered five open-ended questions. The definitions of the five components of transformational leadership measured on the MLQ were turned into these five open-ended questions:

1. When you think about how you have been a role model for your followers, so that they want to emulate you, what tangible things have you done that seem to have worked?

2. When you think about how you have developed trust and confidence among your employees so that they count on you to do the right thing through high ethical and moral standards, what tangible things have you done that seem to have worked?

3. When you think about how you have motivated and inspired followers to commit to the vision of the organization and created a strong sense of purpose among employees, what tangible things have you done that seem to have worked?

4. When you think about how you have encouraged team spirit and provided meaning and challenge to your followers' work, what tangible things have you done that seem to have worked?

5. When you think about how you have encouraged innovation and creativity and promoted critical thinking and problem solving in your followers, what tangible things have you done that seem to have worked?

Results

Overall, those leaders attending the training were comparable to MLQ norms for transformational leadership (M = 2.9, SD = 0.6), transactional leadership (M = 2.3, SD = 0.7) and passive leadership (M = 0.7, SD = 0.3). On the Satisfaction with Supervision scale of the AJIG, the participants scored higher than national norms. The national norm is (M = 38); the participant mean was 47.6.

To understand differences in language used to describe how these leaders engaged in aspects of transformational leadership, a content analysis was done on the responses to the open-ended questions. Content analysis is a technique that utilizes a specific set of procedures for making valid inferences from text (Weber, 1990). Franfort-Nachmias and Nachmias (2000) identified it as "any technique for making inferences by systematically and objectively identifying specific characteristics of messages" (p. 296). Corsini (2002) brought all of these definitions together in one stating the content analysis is "a systematic quantitative procedure of analyzing conceptual material (articles, speeches, films) by determining the frequency of specific ideas, concepts, or terms" (p. 215).

For the first analysis, the participant responses were separated into two groups— those whose 360 MLQ transformational scores were above class mean and those whose transformational scores were lower than the class mean. Based on those two groups, comparisons were made on the frequency of words used in the open-ended responses. Results are displayed in Table 1.

For the second analysis, the participant responses were separated into two groups—those whose 360 ADJI Satisfaction with Supervision scores were above the class mean and those whose Satisfaction with Supervision scores were lower than the class mean. Based on those two groups, comparisons were made on the frequency of words used in the open-ended responses. Results are displayed in Table 2.

Discussion

While both intuition and prior research (Bligh et al., 2004; Burleson, 1987; Caroseli, 2005; Conger, 1991; Flauto, 1999; Hackman & Johnson, 2000; Insch et al., 1997;

Table 1. Differences in the Frequency of Words Used Based on Transformational Leadership Ratings

Words Used More Frequently By Leaders
Below the Group Mean for Transformational Leadership

	Chi^2	P (2-tails)
Don't	46.46	0.00
Schedule	26.67	0.00
Tell	21.70	0.00
Time	13.38	0.00
Focused	13.33	0.00
Instead	13.33	0.00
Performance	9.34	0.01
More	8.51	0.01
Employee	7.35	0.03

Words Used More Frequently By Leaders
Above the Group Mean for Transformational Leadership

	Chi^2	P (2-tails)
Encourage	19.39	0.00
Fun	13.50	0.00
Future	10.80	0.01
Effort	10.00	0.01
Expected	10.00	0.01
Order	10.00	0.01
Plan	10.00	0.01
Listen	9.01	0.01
Discussion	8.10	0.02
Teammates	8.10	0.02
Behind	6.67	0.04
Consistency	6.67	0.04
Results	6.41	0.04
Asking	5.40	0.05
Brainstorm	5.40	0.05
Educate	5.40	0.05
Forum	5.40	0.05
Honesty	5.40	0.05
Innovative	5.40	0.05
Integrity	5.40	0.05
Openly	5.40	0.05
Peer	5.40	0.05
Promote	5.40	0.05
Sincere	5.40	0.05
Solutions	5.40	0.05
Visions	5.40	0.05

Table 2. Differences in the Frequency of Words Used Based on Satisfaction with Supervision Leadership Ratings

Words Used More Frequently By Leaders
Below the Group Mean for Satisfaction with Supervision

	Chi^2	P (2-tails)
Project	31.59	0.00
Work	15.79	0.00
Schedule	15.50	0.00
Detail	13.33	0.00
Initiatives	13.33	0.00
Subordinates	13.33	0.00
Charge	10.00	0.01
Direct	10.00	0.01
Managers	10.00	0.01
Remind	10.00	0.01
Important	9.34	0.01
Performance	9.34	0.01
I	8.96	0.00
Necessary	7.35	0.03
Meetings	6.72	0.04
Agendas	6.67	0.04
Deadline	6.67	0.04
Directly	6.67	0.04
Efforts	6.67	0.04
Formal	6.67	0.04
End	6.41	0.04
Maintain	6.41	0.04
My	5.45	0.05

Words Used More Frequently By Leaders
Above the Group Mean for Satisfaction with Supervision

	Chi^2	P (2-tails)
Show	18.44	0.00
Explain	14.24	0.00
Give	13.70	0.00
Fun	13.50	0.00
Guidance	8.10	0.02
Innovation	8.10	0.02
Smile	8.10	0.02
Honest	6.81	0.03
Truth	5.40	0.05
Bonus	5.40	0.05

(continued)

Words Used More Frequently By Leaders
Above the Group Mean for Satisfaction with Supervision
(continued)

	Chi^2	P (2-tails)
Enthusiasm	5.40	0.05
Family	5.40	0.07
Helping	5.40	0.05
Helps	5.40	0.05
Leader	5.40	0.05
Openly	5.40	0.05
Peer	5.40	0.07
Rewards	5.40	0.07
Sincere	5.40	0.07
Surprise	5.40	0.07

Sypher & Zorn, 1986; Thayer, 1988; Zorn, 1991) suggest the importance of a leader's use of language in conveying leadership style to followers, there is presently a lack of published research that empirically addresses this topic. The current study used content analysis to examine the relationship between usage of particular word units and both leadership style and effectiveness ratings for a group of executives within the context of a leadership development program.

Overall, results indicated that the sample in this study was representative of the general population with respect to the degrees of transformational, transactional, and passive leadership styles. However, this sample scored higher than national norms with respect to the Satisfaction with Supervision scale of the AJIG. Taken together, this can be interpreted as evidence that the importance of the leader-follower relationship is recognized in the corporate community.

The analysis of the actual words used by the leaders in this sample support the idea that both leaders who are more transformational, and more effective (as measured through satisfaction of followers), utilize language differently and, in fact, they use significantly more words associated with the characteristics of a transformational leader.

When reflecting on the language that leaders might use in order to build bridges among followers, words such as *encourage, teammates, brainstorm, educated, honesty, innovative, openly, peer* and *visions* likely increase bridges. In this study, those leaders higher in transformational ratings used more of these bridging type words than did their less transformational counterparts. Conversely, those leaders who were rated lower on transformational leadership used words such as *tell, time, schedule, perfor-*

mance, more and *instead.* These words tend to connote compliance and individual work rather than teamwork and unity.

More studies are needed to see if these results would generalize to a more diverse group of leaders, but the present study undoubtedly serves to offer empirical evidence for implications that have long been put forth in the leadership literature regarding the importance of the specific rhetoric used in the dyadic relationship between leaders and followers.

REFERENCES

Barbuto, J. E., Jr., Fritz, S. M., & Matkin, G. S. (2001). Leaders' bases of social power and anticipation of target's resistance as predictors of transactional and transformational leadership. *Psychological Reports, 89,* 663–666.

Bass, B. M. (1990). *Bass & Stogdill's handbook of leadership* (3rd ed.). New York: The Free Press.

Bass, B. M., & Avolio, B. J. (1994). *Improving organizational effectiveness through transformational leadership.* Thousand Oaks, CA: Sage Publications.

Bass, B. M. & Avolio, B. (2000). *Manual for the Multifactor Leadership Questionnaire, technical report for MLQ Form 5X-short* (2nd ed.). Redwood City, CA: Mindgarden Publishers Inc.

Bligh, M. C., Kohles, J. C., & Meindl, J. R. (2004). Charting the language of leadership: A methodological investigation of President Bush and the crisis of 9/11. *Journal of Applied Psychology, 89,* 562–574.

Bunker, B. B. (1986). *Management training in Japan: Lessons for America.* OD Network Conference, New York, NY, pp. 182–189.

Burleson, B. R. (1987). Cognitive complexity and person centered communication: A review of methods, findings, and explanations. In J. C. McCroskey & J. A. Daly (Eds.), *Personality and interpersonal communication* (pp. 305–349). Beverly Hills, CA: Sage Publications.

Calder, B. J. (1977). An attribution theory of leadership. In B. Staw & G. Salancik (Eds.), *New directions in organizational behavior* (pp. 179–204). Chicago: St. Clair Press.

Caroseli, M. (2005). *The language of leadership.* Amherst, MA: HRD Press.

Clutterback, D., & Hirst, S. (2002). Leadership communication: A status report. *Journal of Communication Management, 6,* 351–354.

Conger, J. (1991). Inspiring others: The language of leadership. *Academy of Management Executives, 5,* 31–45.

Corsini, R. (2002). *The dictionary of psychology.* New York: Brunner-Routledge.

DeSteno, D., Petty, R. E., Rucker, D. D., Wegener, D. T., & Braverman, J. (2004). Discrete emotions and persuasion: The role of emotion-induced expectancies. *Journal of Personality and Social Psychology, 86,* 3514–3536.

Eden, D., & Leviathan, U. (1975). Implicit leadership theory as a determinant of the factor structure underlying supervisory behavior. *Journal of Applied Psychology, 60,* 736–741.

Felfe, J., & Schyns, B. (2006). Personality and the perception of transformational leadership: The impact of extraversion, neuroticism, personal need for structure, and occupational self-efficacy. *Journal of Applied Social Psychology, 36,* 708–739.

Fiedler, F. E. (1967). *A theory of leadership effectiveness.* New York: McGraw-Hill.

Flauto, F. J. (1999). Walking the talk: The relationship between leadership and communication competence. *The Journal of Leadership Studies, 6,* 86–89.

Frankfort-Nachmias, C., & Nachmias, D. (2000). *Research methods in the social sciences* (6th ed.). New York: Worth Publishers.

French, J. R. P., & Raven, B. (1959). The bases of social power. In D. Cartwright (Ed.), *Studies in social power* (pp. 150–167). Ann Arbor: University of Michigan Press.

George, J. M. (2000). Emotions and leadership: The role of emotional intelligence. *Human Relations, 53,* 1027–1055.

Graen, G., & Cashman, J. F. (1975). A role-making model of leadership in formal organizations: A developmental approach. In J. G. Hunt & L. L. Larson (Eds.), *Leadership frontiers* (pp. 143–165). Kent, OH: Kent State University Press.

Hackman, M. Z., & Johnson, C. E. (2000). *Leadership: A communication perspective.* Prospect Heights, IL: Waveland Press.

Hersey, P., & Blanchard, K. H. (1969). Life-cycle theory of leadership. *Training and Development Journal, 23,* 26–34.

Hollander, E. P., & Julian, J. W. (1969). Contemporary trends in the analysis of leadership processes. *Psychological Bulletin, 71,* 387–397.

House, R. J. (1976). A 1976 theory of charismatic leadership effectiveness. In J. G. Hunt & L. L. Larson (Eds.), *Leadership: The cutting edge.* Carbondale: Southern Illinois University Press.

Insch, G. S., Moore, J. E., & Murphey, L. D. (1997). Content analysis in leadership research: Examples, procedures, and suggestions for future use. *The Leadership Quarterly, 8,* 1–25.

Johnson, C., Vinson, L., Hackman, M., & Hardin, T. (1989). The effects of an instructor's use of hesitation forms on student ratings of quality, recommendations to hire, and lecture listening. *Journal of the International Listening Association, 3,* 32–43.

Kelloway, E. K., & Barling, J. (1993). Members' participation in local union activities: Measurement, prediction, and replication. *Journal of Applied Psychology, 78,* 262–279.

Kennedy, G. A. (1994). *A new history of classical rhetoric.* Princeton, NJ: Princeton University Press.

Lord, R. (1977). Functional leadership behavior: Measurement and relation to social power and leadership perceptions. *Administrative Science Quarterly, 22,* 402–410.

Lord, R. (1985). An information processing approach to social perceptions, leadership, and behavioral measurement in organizations. In B. M. Staw & L. L. Cummings (Eds.), *Research in organizational behavior* (pp. 87–128). Greenwich, CT: JAI.

Lord, R., DeVader, C., & Alliger, G. (1986). A meta-analysis of the relation between personality traits and leadership perceptions: An application of validity generalization procedures. *Journal of Applied Psychology, 71,* 402–410.

Lord, R., Foti, R., & DeVader, C. (1984). A test of leadership categorization theory: Internal structure, information processing, and leadership perceptions. *Organizational Behavior and Human Performance, 34,* 343–378.

Lord, R., & Maher, K. (1990). Perceptions of leadership and their implications in organizations. In J. S. Carroll (Ed.), *Applied social psychology and organizational settings* (pp. 129–154). Hillsdale, NJ: Lawrence Erlbaum Associates.

Lord, R., & Maher, K. (1991). *Leadership and information processing.* Boston: Routledge.

Mann, R. D. (1959). A review of the relationship between personality and performance in small groups. *Psychological Bulletin, 56,* 241–270.

Mischel, W. (1977). The interaction of person and situation. In D. Magnusson & N. S. Endler (Eds.), *Personality at the crossroads: Current issues in interactional psychology* (pp. 333–352). Hillsdale, NJ: Lawrence Erlbaum Associates.

Phillips, J. S., & Lord, R. (1981). Causal attributions and perceptions of leadership. *Administrative Science Quarterly, 30,* 143–163.

Riggio, R. E., Riggio, H. R., Salinas, C., & Cole, E. J. (2003). The role of social and emotional communication skills in leader emergence and effectiveness. *Group Dynamics: Theory, Research, and Practice, 7*, 83–103.

Russell, S. S., Spitzmuller, L. F., Stanton, J. M., Smith, P. C., & Ironson, G. H. (2004). Shorter can also be better: The abridged job in general scale. *Educational and Psychological Measurement, 64*(5), 878–893.

Salter, C. R., Green, M., & Ree, M. (2006, April). *A study of the relationship between followers' personality and leadership ratings of George W. Bush.* Paper presented at the meeting of the Midwest Political Science Association on Personality and Patriotism.

Stanton, J. M. (2000). Empirical distributions of correlations as a tool for scale reduction. *Behavior Research Methods, Instruments, & Computers, 32*(3), 403–406.

Stanton, J., Sinar, E., Blazer, W., & Smith, P. (2002). Issues and strategies for reducing self-report scales. *Personal Psychology, 55*, 167–193.

Stogdill, R. M. (1948). Personal factors associated with leadership: A survey of the literature. *The Journal of Psychology, 25*, 35–71.

Sypher, B. D. (1981). The importance of social cognitive abilities in organizations. In R. Bostrom (Ed.), *Competence in communication* (pp. 103–128). Beverly Hills, CA: Sage Publications.

Sypher, B. D., & Zorn, T. E. (1986). Communicated related abilities and upward mobility: A longitudinal investigation. *Human Communication Research, 12*, 420–431.

Thayer, L. (1988). Leadership/communication: A critical review and a modest proposal. In G. M. Goldhaber & G. A. Barnett (Eds.), *Handbook of organizational communication* (pp. 231–263). Norwood, NJ: Ablex.

Weber, R. P. (1990). *Basic content analysis: Vol. quantitative applications in the social sciences* (2nd ed.). Newbury Park, CA: Sage Publications.

Winter, L., & Uleman, J. S. (1984). When are social judgments made? Evidence for the spontaneousness of trait inferences. *Journal of Personality and Social Psychology, 47*, 237–252.

Zorn, T. E. (1991). Construct system development, transformational leadership, and leadership messages. *Southern Communication Journal, 56*, 178–193.

CHARLES SALTER is an Assistant Professor of Business at Schreiner University. Dr. Salter holds a PhD in leadership studies from Our Lady of the Lake University and an MBA from the University of Houston.

MEGHAN CARMODY-BUBB is an Assistant Professor of Leadership at Our Lady of the Lake University. She holds a PhD in experimental psychology from Texas Tech University.

PHYLLIS DUNCAN is an Assistant Professor of Leadership at Our Lady of the Lake University. She holds a PhD in organizational leadership from the University of the Incarnate Word, an MBA from the University of Arkansas, and an MS from Southwest University.

MARK GREEN is a Professor of Leadership at Our Lady of the Lake University. He holds a PhD in educational administration from the American University, an MEd from the University of Missouri, an MS from the American University, and an MBA from Our Lady of the Lake University.

Two Trains Running: Tolstoy on Lincoln and Leadership

By Norman W. Provizer

WHILE A GUEST OF A TRIBAL CHIEF IN THE CAUCASUS, LEO TOLSTOY is asked to recount some tales of great figures in history. In response, the famed Russian novelist, according to an interview in a 1909 issue of the New York newspaper *The World*, tells the gathered clan of rulers and military leaders, including the Czars and Napoleon. "But," the tribal chief of the Circassians says after hearing Tolstoy's stories, "you have not told us a syllable about the greatest general and greatest ruler of the world. We want to know something about him. He was a hero. He spoke with a voice of thunder; he laughed like the sunrise and his deeds were strong as a rock. . . . His name was Lincoln and the country in which he lived is called America, which is so far away that if a youth should journey to reach it he would be an old man when he arrived. Tell us of that man" (Stakelberg, 1909, pp. 1–2).

In the account published just days before the centennial of Lincoln's birth, Tolstoy complies with the request and notes, "This little incident proves how largely the name of Lincoln is worshipped throughout the world and how legendary his personality has become." Because, in Tolstoy's view, Lincoln was neither an outstanding general nor the most skillful of statesmen, the novelist asks, "Now, why was Lincoln so great that he overshadows all other national heroes?" Then Tolstoy answers his question by saying of Lincoln that "his supremacy expresses itself altogether in his particular moral power and in the greatness of his character. . . . Lincoln was bigger than his country—bigger than all the Presidents together. We are still too near to his greatness, but after a few centuries more our posterity will find him considerably bigger than we do. His genius is still too strong and too powerful for the common understanding, just as the sun is too hot when its light beams directly on us" (Stakelberg, 1909, pp. 1–2). For Tolstoy, as long as the world exists, Lincoln's universal example of greatness, as a humanitarian and a prophet of freedom, will live—and not just in the American memory (Goodwin, 2005, pp. 747–748; Peterson, 1994, pp. 186, 396).

Tolstoy's choice of the terms *moral power* and *character* to explain Lincoln's cherished place in history as an "ageless and universal standard" is not surprising (Davies, 1987, p. 332). In an article that first appeared in the Finnish journal *Progress* prior to its publication in *The World*, for example, the novelist wrote, "The only government in which I believe is that which exercises a *moral authority*. Moses, Buddha, Christ are the great law-givers, the real autocrats, who ruled not by force, but by *character*, whose government was one of love, justice, and brotherhood" (Tolstoy, 1909, emphasis added). And for Tolstoy, Lincoln was, in fact, "a Christ in miniature, a saint of humanity" (Stakelberg, 1909, p. 1). In the eyes of the novelist, when compared to other historic figures, Lincoln emerges as "the only real giant in depth of feeling and in certain moral power. . . . He was the one who wanted to be great through his smallness. . . . He wanted to be himself in the world, not the world in himself" (Stakelberg, 1909, p. 2).

> **'THE ONLY GOVERNMENT IN WHICH I BELIEVE,' LEO TOLSTOY SAID, 'IS THAT WHICH EXERCISES A *MORAL AUTHORITY*.'**

Of course, even such excessive praise of Lincoln is not at all unique. So what is it about Tolstoy's words that should capture our attention? Simply put, the answer to that question revolves around the role the Russian author occupies in the study of leadership as the favored counterweight to Thomas Carlyle and the great man theory of history. After all, it was Tolstoy who proclaimed, "Heroes—that's a lie and invention; there are simply people, people and nothing else" (Bloom, 1994, p. 344). It seems there are two trains running out of the Tolstoy station, each on its own set of tracks and moving in opposite directions. Despite the view that "there are simply people, people and nothing else," Tolstoy's description of Lincoln tells a different story as well—a story well worth exploring.

II

"However well-intentioned," Warren Bennis reminds us, "those who write about leadership have tended to become embroiled in one or more of the now familiar controversies on the subject" (Bennis, 1997, p. 22). The first such debate for Bennis "is whether leaders are larger-than-life figures—heroes who can change the weather, as Winston Churchill said his ancestor John Churchill could—or embodiments of forces greater than themselves. I think of this as a debate between Tolstoy and Carlyle. . . . To use a metaphor that might have left Tolstoy tugging his beard in confusion, the leader in Tolstoy's view is just another surfer riding the waves of the zeitgeist, albeit the surfer with the biggest board." In contrast, Carlyle "argues that every institution is the lengthened shadow of a great man. Had he been a Southern Californian, he might have written that great leaders don't just ride waves, they make them" (Bennis, 1997, p. 22).

University of Southern California President Steven Sample adds that in a course he teaches with Bennis, they contrast the views of Tolstoy, "who believed that history shapes and determines leaders," with those of Carlyle, "who believed that leaders shape and determine history" (Sample, 2003, p. 191). And on that front, Sample, like many others, charts a middle course, writing, "It may well be that our world is largely Tolstoyan, subject to historical forces which no man or woman can fully measure and analyze, and the consequences of which no person can fully predict. Thus, to that extent, leaders are in fact history's slaves." Yet, Carlyle's able man "can make a difference in the course of human events; that the decisions of leaders can indeed have a lasting impact on the world; that historical determinism is never totally in control" (Sample, 2003, pp. 191–192). What is interesting is that when it comes to Lincoln, Tolstoy himself appears to chart a middle course between the two paths he and Carlyle have come to represent in the study of leadership.

In this sense, the bipolar approach to leadership framed in terms of Tolstoy and Carlyle has often painted a portrait of the Russian novelist and student of history with too broad a brush. While Tolstoy finds no place in James MacGregor Burns's seminal 1978 study *Leadership*, Burns does consider the novelist in his 2003 book *Transforming Leadership*. There Burns notes, "The most eloquent—and most savage—rebuttal to determinists on the left and the right came not from another philosopher but from a writer who had long pondered the question of historical causation, Leo Tolstoy." In addition to rejecting "as frauds all theories that claimed to disclose history's inner mechanics," Tolstoy also "poured equal scorn on the pretensions of Great Men. Free will was no less a delusion than simple determinism." Instead, reality rests on multiple causation and the more "we delve in search of these causes the more of them we find; and each separate cause or whole series of causes appears to us equally valid in itself and equally false by its insignificance compared to the magnitude of the events." Therefore people might feel they were exercising free will in making history. But that was only "because the causes that in fact determined their actions were infinitesimal and infinite, forever beyond their comprehension." The one certainty is that "none of us, no general, no leader, could control events. Indeed, even the greatest king was only 'history's slave'" (Burns, 2003, pp. 14–15).

On this point, Lincoln appears to agree. When asked to explain the shift from his inaugural pledge not to interfere with slavery to the idea of emancipation, Lincoln wrote in an April 4, 1864, letter to newspaper editor Albert G. Hodges, "I claim not to have controlled events, but confess plainly that events have controlled me." David Herbert Donald uses that frequently cited line as the opening epigram for his 1995 volume *Lincoln* and relates its sentiment to views concerning Lincoln's passivity, fatalism, and the role of Divine purpose (Donald, 1995, pp. 14–15, 514–515).

But such a convergence between Lincoln and the Tolstoy portrayed in much of the literature of leadership studies is not without its ambiguities. True, circumstances made emancipation and the use of African American soldiers, in Lincoln's view, a military necessity that required the action taken. Still, however defined, circumstances never eliminated the ongoing necessity of choice.

Events control actions by providing parameters that shape and channel choice. Yet, the leader, instead of being "history's slave," is in actuality history's servant— and that is something quite different. To borrow from Alexis de Tocqueville's conclusion to *Democracy in America*, "Providence did not make mankind entirely free or completely enslaved. Providence has, in truth, drawn a predestined circle around each man beyond which he cannot pass; but within those vast limits man is strong and free, and so are peoples" (Tocqueville, 1835/1988, p. 705). Later, though from a very different angle, even Karl Marx would note that in the relationship between human agency and systemic structure, "Men make their own history, but they do not make it just as they please; they do not make it under circumstances chosen by themselves, but under circumstances directly encountered, given and transmitted from the past" (Burns, 2003, p. 15).

 THE LEADER, INSTEAD OF BEING "HISTORY'S SLAVE," IS IN ACTUALITY HISTORY'S SERVANT— AND THAT IS SOMETHING QUITE DIFFERENT.

Thus, while Tolstoy is associated with the notion that leaders are the "playthings of massive forces that move history toward unknown and predetermined ends," it is difficult, at best, to see Tolstoy's Lincoln simply as a plaything lacking human agency (Tucker, 1995, p. 27). And it is equally true that despite his expression of being controlled by events, Lincoln agonized over the choices he had to make, adding an important caveat to the very idea of being controlled by those events. As Ralph Waldo Emerson notes in *Representative Men*, even Napoleon, when commenting on his son, said, "My son cannot replace me; and I could not replace myself. I am the creature of circumstances" (Emerson, 1850/1996, p. 133). This from the man whom Paul Johnson describes as "the grandest possible refutation of those determinists who hold that events are governed by forces, classes, economics, and geography rather than by the powerful wills of men and women" (Johnson, 2006, p. ix).

In this sense, while each of us is a "creature of circumstances," politics, nevertheless, remains "a matter of choices from the possibilities offered by a given historical situation and cultural context" (Anderson, 1971, p. 121). As William James noted in an 1880 essay, change emerges from the "acts or the examples of individuals" (Harter, 2006, p. 182). Through those acts and examples, people become, according to Louis Menand's examination of James, "active agents" who have a say "in the evolving constitution of the universe: when we choose a belief and act on it, we change the way things are" (Menand, 2002, p. 220). And when it came to those choices, as Tolstoy recognized, Lincoln (though not in his view Napoleon) stood several standard deviations above the rest.

III

In 1953, Isaiah Berlin produced a slender volume exploring Tolstoy's view of history called *The Hedgehog and the Fox*. The title comes from the Greek poet Archilochus who said, "The fox knows many things, but the hedgehog knows one big thing." From this, Berlin draws his critical distinction between hedgehogs "who relate everything to a single central vision" and foxes "who pursue many ends, often unrelated and even contradictory" (Berlin, 1953/1993, p. 3). After placing numerous figures into either the camp of foxes or that of hedgehogs, Berlin asks where it is that Tolstoy belongs and responds that it is a question with "no clear or immediate answer." In place of that missing answer, Berlin instead offers the hypothesis that the Russian novelist and thinker "was by nature a fox, but believed in being a hedgehog" and that "the conflict between what he was and what he believed emerges nowhere so clearly as in his view of history, to which some of his most brilliant and most paradoxical pages are devoted" (Berlin, 1953/1993, pp. 5–6).

That paradox (Tolstoy's cognitive dissonance, if you will) involves the clash between his insistence that events are variable, based on an apparently infinite number of small causes, and his desire to have an all-embracing and simple vision that defines the order of things. One might say he was a nihilist with an "inability to abide nihilism" (Bloom, 1994, p. 333). In short, Tolstoy's inner fox could not defeat his desire to be a hedgehog, while his desire to be that hedgehog could not overcome his fox-like nature.

Thirty-eight years after Berlin published his Tolstoy study, James McPherson borrowed its basic theme to examine Abraham Lincoln. In McPherson's eyes, Lincoln emerges as "one of the foremost hedgehogs in American history" who, during the Civil War, focused "on one big thing"—preserving the Union both in terms of the nation's fundamental principles and its territorial integrity (McPherson, 1991, pp. 114–115). In praising Lincoln, therefore, Tolstoy could recognize the value of what he himself could never be. Thus while Tolstoy was driven by a desire to penetrate "first causes," Lincoln was able to act knowing the nature of that "first cause" and relating all else to that "single central vision." Berlin's study of Tolstoy, in the words of Michael Ignatieff, "seemed to capture the fissure between Tolstoy's fox-like gift as a novelist for conveying the fine detail of human life and his hedgehog-like search for an overarching theory of human existence" (Ignatieff, 1999, p. 173). If Tolstoy was the fox who wanted to be a hedgehog, Lincoln was the hedgehog who knew how to play the role of the fox without ever becoming one. You might say, in this regard, that he was either a "fox-hog" or a "hedge-fox," to borrow the hybrid terms used by Philip Tetlock in his examination of the cognitive-style correlates of good judgment exercised by experts involved in forecasting (Tetlock, 2006, pp. 72–77).

" " IN PRAISING LINCOLN, TOLSTOY COULD RECOGNIZE THE VALUE OF WHAT HE HIMSELF COULD NEVER BE.

As such, Lincoln could transform and transact without ever confusing the two. Girded by humility, along with talent, he displayed "how a powerful, even superior person could nevertheless open himself to others, could learn as well as teach, could nurture as well as direct" and thereby become "the best model Americans have of democratic leadership" (Miroff, 1993, pp. 122, 124). Leadership that considers not only what we ought to be but also "what we are and what we may become" (Maude, 1975, p. 213). Leadership that accepts responsibility for the choices made while recognizing just how much there is that lies beyond its control and, perhaps, beyond the control of anyone (Fuller, 2000, p. 5). That is, leadership that faces up to, in Virgil's phrase from the *Aeneid*, the *lachrymae rerum*—the "tears of things" (Fuller, 2000, p. 4).

IV

In the modern-day study of leadership, there is a clear effort to focus on the subject more as a multivariate process than as a world in which discrete individuals play a distinct and determinate role (Barker, 2002). Thus Tolstoy's view of history often finds an eager audience, despite arguments that his essential approach actually "stands in opposition" to the very notion of leadership studies itself (Harter, 2006, p. 35). As the novelist notes in his extended epilogue to *War and Peace*, "The life of nations is not contained in the life of a few men. . . ." (Tolstoy, 1865/2002, p. 1360). And, like Tolstoy, many contemporary writers on leadership are "irritated by references to the dominant influence of great men or of ideas" (Berlin, 1953/1993, p. 25). In both cases, the notion "that individuals can, by the use of their own resources, understand and control the course of events" is nothing less than the greatest of illusions (Berlin, 1953/ 1993, p. 20). "To history," Tolstoy writes, "the recognition of the free wills of men as forces able to influence historical events, that is, not subjects to laws, is the same as would be to astronomy the recognition of free will in the movements of the heavenly bodies" (Tolstoy, 1865/2002, p. 1383).

Yet, despite such protestations, a number of Tolstoy's Russian critics point out that the novelist's characters (his theory aside) "are real and not mere pawns in the hands of unintelligible destiny ... individual wills may not be all-powerful, but neither are they totally impotent, and some are more effective than others" (Berlin, 1953/1993, pp. 33, 35).

In fact, writing in his diary in 1909, Tolstoy noted that mankind progresses "because people of advanced views change the environment little by little, pointing the way to an eternally remote state of perfection" (Tolstoy, 1985, p. 599). And following that path, Tolstoy scholar Donna Tussing Orwin argues that the novelist, especially later in his life, was determined to become "an example of upright conduct"—a determination based on his belief that "individuals rather than institutions introduce transcendental truths into the world and nourish them" (Orwin, 2002, p. 235).

Importantly, she continues, "Tolstoy may have modeled his own activity partly on the English essayist Thomas Carlyle's notion of the hero. He read at least parts of Carlyle's *On Heroes* in the 1850s, and was a great admirer of Carlyle in later life" (Orwin, 1996, pp. 63–70; Orwin, 2002, p. 235). As the novelist informs us in a 1904 diary entry, he was reading "Amiel, Carlyle, and Mazzini" (Tolstoy, 1985, p. 528). Therefore, simply defining him as the antipode to Carlyle won't quite do.

Additionally, if one accepts Boris Eikhenbaum's proposition that "what oppressed Tolstoy most was his lack of positive convictions" (Berlin, 1953/1993, p. 37), then what might well have attracted him most to Lincoln was that the American leader, whatever his inner ghosts, was not at all lacking in such conviction. That theme finds further reinforcement in the last novel written by Tolstoy—a novel that returns us to the Caucasus.

Hadji Murád was posthumously published in 1912, two years after Tolstoy's death (Tolstoy, 1912/2005). Tolstoy's link to Hadji Murád, the Avar chieftan around whom the book revolves, went back in 1851 and he began work on it in 1896, producing multiple drafts into 1905. The result is a slender novel that critic Harold Bloom refers to as the "best story in the world, or at least the best that I have ever read" (Bloom, 1994, p. 336).

Murád "lives and dies as the archaic epic hero" and, in so doing, he represents "the best there is in his universe—whether Caucasian or Russian—at every attribute

that matters: daring, horsemanship, resourcefulness, leadership, vision of reality."
When he dies, he does so courageously with "his identity not only unimpaired but
enhanced" (Bloom, 1994, pp. 349, 344). What more could a hero be?

Significantly, Tolstoy was aware of his own internal conflicts on such matters.
While he was producing the drafts of the book, the novelist told his daughter he was
writing it "on the quiet," ashamed of himself for the very act of creating it. After all,
"its subject matter and his treatment of it run directly counter to his professed belief
in the doctrine of non-resistance, and his appeal to men to love their enemies and to
turn the other cheek" (Christian, 1969, p. 240). Once again, we are reminded that
Tolstoy's desire to be a hedgehog could not banish his inner fox.

**   “ “   TOLSTOY'S DESIRE TO BE A HEDGEHOG   ” ”**
COULD NOT BANISH HIS INNER FOX.

Seen in this light, Murád, like Lincoln, further accentuates the positions
occupied by the "hero" in Tolstoy's thought, denied and yet revered. And in the
existence of such contradictions, there lies a cautionary message for those who would
prefer to see leadership only in terms of a process, devoid of any substantial direction
and purpose derived from the internal and external worlds of the individual men and
women we call leaders. The world is, certainly, far too complex a place to explain
through a limited set of biographies (Pfeffer, 1977). Yet, neither can those biographies
simply be ignored.

"The pendulum," in Jerrold Post's words, "that overswung from the view of
history as consequence of power, ignoring the role of leadership, to the 'great man'
theory of history, which emphasized the centrality of leadership, has come to rest with
the current working model, the leader in context" (Post, 2004, p. 13). That was the
Lincoln praised by Tolstoy.

V

In a set of historiometric inquiries that appeared under the title of *Genius, Creativity,
and Leadership*, Dean Keith Simonton empirically compared Tolstoy's stated view
"that the will of the historic hero does not control the actions of the mass, but is itself
continually controlled" (Simonton, 1984, p. 135) to Carlyle's notion of great men as
"the modellers, patterns, and in the wide sense the creators, of whatsoever the general
mass of men contrived to do or to attain" (Carlyle, 1841/1966, p. 1). Training his
quantitative guns on Napoleon to examine this debate (though Carlyle actually
considered Bonaparte as much a "quack" and "charlatan" as a hero), Simonton
discovers that both sides "have some merit" depending on the factors examined. He

thus concludes, "The reality of the matter is much too complicated to assign victory to either theorist. On the battlefield, at least, Carlyle and Tolstoy have fought to a draw, neither managing to conquer the explanatory domains of his adversary" (Simonton, 1984, pp. 152–153, 155).

Of course, Simonton might have added that with Tolstoy, the novelist's explanatory domain itself is filled with complications and contradictions. Still, the proclamation of a draw regarding Napoleon underscores the importance of Tolstoy's comments on Lincoln, highlighting, as they do, the significance of "the leader in context." Just as the leader cannot totally obliterate context, neither can context completely eliminate the impact of the leader. Like good generals, good leaders "do make a difference" and success in the political as well as the military arena often "goes to the side which is well led" even if the attempt to explain all failures "as the fault of individual commanders will not do" (Cohen & Gooch, 2006, pp. 231–232).

In exercising supreme command, the hedgehog Lincoln did more than find the right generals, he also provided "constant oversight of the war effort from beginning to end" (Cohen, 2003, p. 17). And he did that with the kind of character and moral power that captured the Russian novelist. After all is said and done, Tolstoy, despite his meta-view of the nature of historical events, understood that who Lincoln was mattered.

"No matter how vital we think the role of leadership in the rise of a mass movement," Eric Hoffer reminded us midway through the twentieth century that "there is no doubt that the leader cannot create the conditions which make the rise of a movement possible. He cannot conjure a movement out of the void." Yet, Hoffer continued, "once the stage is set, the presence of an outstanding leader is indispensable. Without him there will be no movement" (Hoffer, 1951, pp. 103–104). In this regard, when it comes to Lincoln, one part of Tolstoy certainly seems to agree.

REFERENCES

Anderson, C. (1971). Comparative policy analysis. *Comparative Politics, 4*(1), 117–131.

Barker, R. (2002). *On the nature of leadership*. Lanham, MD: University Press of America.

Bennis, W. (1997). *Managing people is like herding cats*. Provo, UT: Executive Excellence Publishing.

Berlin, I. (1993). *The hedgehog and the fox*. Chicago: Ivan Dees Publisher. Originally published in 1953.

Bloom, H. (1994). *The Western canon*. New York: Harcourt Brace.

Burns, J. M. (2003). *Transforming leadership*. New York: Atlantic Monthly Press.

Carlyle, T. (1966). *On heroes, hero-worship and the heroic in history*. Edited by Carl Niemeyer. Lincoln, NE: University of Nebraska Press. Originally published in 1841.

Christian, R. F. (1969). *Tolstoy: A critical introduction*. Cambridge, UK: Cambridge University Press.

Cohen, E. (2003). *Supreme command: Soldiers, statesmen, and leadership in wartime*. New York: Anchor Books.

Cohen, E., & Gooch, J. (2006). *Military misfortunes: The anatomy of failure in war*. New York: Free Press.

Davies, J. C. (1987). Lincoln: The saint and the man. In W. Pederson & A. McLaurin (Eds.), *The rating game in American politics*. New York: Irvington Publishers.

Donald, D. H. (1995). *Lincoln*. New York: Simon and Schuster.

Emerson, R. W. (1996). *Representative men: Seven lectures*. Cambridge, MA: Harvard University Press. Originally published in 1850.

Fuller, T. (2000). *Leading and leadership*. Notre Dame, IN: University of Notre Dame Press.

Goodwin, D. K. (2005). *Team of rivals: The political genius of Abraham Lincoln*. New York: Simon and Schuster.

Harter, N. (2006). *Clearings in the forest: On the study of leadership*. West Lafayette, IN: Purdue University Press.

Hoffer, E. (1951). *The true believer*. New York: Harper and Brothers.

Ignatieff, M. (1999). *Isaiah Berlin: A life*. New York: Henry Holt/Owl Books.

Johnson, P. (2006). *Napoleon*. New York: Penguin Books.

Maude, A. (1975). *Leo Tolstoy*. New York: Haskell House Publishers.

McPherson, J. (1991). *Abraham Lincoln and the second American revolution*. New York: Oxford University Press.

Menand, L. (2002). *The metaphysical club*. New York: Farrar, Straus and Giroux.

Miroff, B. (1993). *Icons of democracy*. New York: Basic Books.

Orwin, D. T. (1996). Tolstoy and patriotism. In A. Donskov & J. Woodsworth (Eds.), *Lev Tolstoy and the concept of brotherhood*. Ottawa, Canada: Legas.

Orwin, D. T. (2002). Courage in Tolstoy. In D. T. Orwin (Ed.), *The Cambridge companion to Tolstoy*. Cambridge, UK: Cambridge University Press.

Pfeffer, J. (1977). The ambiguity of leadership. *Academy of Management Review, 2*(1), 104–112.

Peterson, M. (1994). *Lincoln in American memory*. New York: Oxford University Press.

Post, J. (2004). *Leaders and followers in a dangerous world*. Ithaca, NY: Cornell University Press.

Sample, S. (2003). *The contrarian's guide to leadership*. San Francisco: Jossey-Bass.

Simonton, D. K. (1984). *Genius, creativity, and leadership: Historiometric inquiries*. Cambridge, MA: Harvard University Press.

Stakelberg, S. (1909, February 7). Tolstoi holds Lincoln world's greatest hero. *The World* (New York). Front-page story based on an interview with Tolstoy about Lincoln.

Tetlock, P. (2006). *Expert political judgment*. Princeton, NJ: Princeton University Press.

Tocqueville, A. de (1988). *Democracy in America*. Translated by G. Lawrence and edited by J. P. Mayer. New York: Perennial Library. Originally published in 1835 (Volume One) and 1840 (Volume Two).

Tolstoy, L. (1909, February 7). Tolstoi compares America and Europe. *The World* (New York). Editorial section. Available digitally from the American Newspaper Repository at http://home.gwi.net/~dnb/tolstoy/tolstoy.htm

Tolstoy, L. (1985). *Tolstoy's diaries, volume II*. Edited and translated by R. F. Christian. New York: Scribner's.

Tolstoy, L. (2002). *War and peace*. Translated by C. Garnett. New York: Modern Library. Originally published 1865–1869.

Tolstoy, L. (2005). *Hadji Murád*. Translated by A. Maude. New York: Barnes and Noble. Originally published in 1912.

Tucker, R. (1995). *Politics as leadership*. Columbia: University of Missouri Press.

NORMAN W. PROVIZER is the director of the Golda Meir Center for Political Leadership and a professor of political science at Metropolitan State College of Denver. He received his PhD from the University of Pennsylvania, and most recently coedited *Leaders of the Pack: Polls and Case Studies of Great Supreme Court Justices*.

Developing Leaders for Sustainable Development

An Investigation into the Impact and Outcomes of a UK-Based Master's Programme

By Gareth Edwards, Sharon Turnbull, David Stephens, and Andy Johnston

> …integrating sustainability thinking and practice into organizational structure is not a trivial task and requires a vision, commitment and leadership.
>
> Azapagic (2003, p. 303)

IN AN INTERVIEW BEFORE HIS UNTIMELY DEATH, THE MANAGEMENT scholar Sumantra Ghoshal suggested that many management practices that have evolved in the last two and a half decades have had little regard for concepts such as sustainable development (Bernhut, 2004). Indeed, organisations seem to lack leaders with a vision for sustainability (Giampalmi, 2004) and UK business schools pay little attention to issues surrounding sustainable development (Coopey, 2003). From a more general perspective it has been suggested that for society to accept transition to a sustainable agenda there needs to be a change in the mind-set and values of society's leaders, and that the logical source of this change is higher education (Johnson & Beloff, 1998). A UK-based master's programme, provided by a charitable organisation based in the UK called Forum for the Future, is tackling this shortfall.

The master's course in Leadership for Sustainable Development has been running since 1996 and defines sustainable development as "A dynamic process which enables all people to realise their potential and improve their quality of life in ways which simultaneously protect and enhance the Earth's life support systems" (Forum for the Future, 2007). The programme has three core elements:

- Academic understanding of leadership and sustainability
- Work-based learning involving high-level placements in six sectors of society: environmental or development campaigning organisations, national government, local or regional government, business, finance or regulatory institutions, and media
- Skills and personal development based around leadership development and team-building

All three areas constitute a circular experiential learning process which involves project work (management simulations, problem-solving and decision-making tasks, as well as work-based projects), facilitated review (centred on exploring feelings and emotions to develop emotional intelligence), and theoretical input (academic lectures and coursework).

The programme has now had over 100 graduates working in a diverse range of organisations ranging from large blue-chip companies to governmental and community organisations. The main thread of the programme is a series of challenging placements undertaken within a wide range of organisations—each one designed to stimulate reflection on practice and catalyse learning from experiencing new and diverse settings. Early in the programme, each cohort of twelve also attends an experiential leadership development course designed to stimulate self and team reflection, and to provoke deeper understanding of the practice of leadership. The programme's purpose has been to develop knowledgeable and purposeful leaders who will make a real impact on the sustainability agenda.

Other programmes offering formal education on leadership and sustainable development are available (e.g., Johnson & Beloff, 1998; Shinn, 2005). There is, however, a lack of evidence as to how much these programmes have an impact on students. The research reported in this paper addresses this dearth by conducting a qualitative study into how a programme of this nature has impacted on participants.

Research Aims

This paper focuses on the benefits of the programme for the participants in terms of their ability to operate successfully in their chosen work and make a contribution to the sustainable development agenda. Leadership, in particular, is regarded as vital in building a sustainable future into the twenty-first century, and this leadership should have a working knowledge of various functions *of* and *in* organisations and an understanding of the relationships between these functions (Giampalmi, 2004; Reid, Scott, & Gough, 2002; Welford & Ytterhus, 2004). This is important given the argument that being proactive with respect to sustainable development may mean different things in different organizational contexts (Vredenburg & Westley, 1999).

Recent research reported by Burgoyne (2006) has suggested that leadership development has three main outcomes: confidence, pause for reflection, and networking. This research had the opportunity to corroborate these claims. In addition, recent research (Gill & Edwards, 2003; Edwards & Gill, 2005; Edwards & Turnbull, 2005; Turnbull & Edwards, 2005) also suggests that experiential learning does have a positive impact on the development of leadership skills. Indeed, there is evidence that college student leadership can be developed (Zimmerman-Oster & Burkhardt, 1999).

Furthermore, other recent research suggests a combination of work-based learning, conceptual ideas, and social interaction as the basis of effective leadership development (Bentley & Turnbull, 2005). The programme uses a combination of all the above techniques to develop the leadership ability of students with a particular emphasis on sustainable development.

In addition, the literature suggests a model of the change process for sustainability: awareness, agency, and association (Ballard, 2005). *Awareness* refers to the awareness of what is happening and what is required, *agency* refers to the ability to find a response that seems personally meaningful, and *association* refers to association with other people in groups and networks. This research also considered this model in evaluating the level of impact graduates were having on the sustainability agenda.

Research Methodology

The research was designed to evaluate outcomes of the programme at the individual level. Outcomes evaluation focuses on changes in attitudes, perspectives, behaviour, knowledge, skills, status, or level of functioning (Marzano, 1993; Schalock, 2001; Stake, 1967; W. G. Kellogg Foundation, 1998, 2002).

This study has used an inductive approach. We elicited autobiographical stories from fifteen interviewees and two focus group attendees, and having transcribed their stories we analysed and coded these thematically. The interviewees were volunteers who had signed up to be interviewed at the previous alumni event.

Toward the beginning of each interview we asked each interviewee to complete a timeline depicting significant dates and events that they believed had shaped their thinking and actions prior to coming on the course, as well as significant dates and events since leaving the course. The purpose of the timeline was to stimulate memory and reflection in the participants of our study. Our aims were to understand how the participants constructed their choice of this programme, how they saw it fitting into their life trajectories, the triggers which led them to apply for a place, what they hoped to gain, and how their career plans and outcomes had been informed by their participation in the programme.

We also sought to understand how the graduates made sense of the experiences they encountered during the course of the programme itself, and the impact of different aspects of the programme on their current thinking and actions.

 LEADERSHIP DEVELOPMENT HAS THREE MAIN OUTCOMES: CONFIDENCE, PAUSE FOR REFLECTION, AND NETWORKING.

The interviews were semi-structured and conducted by three different interviewers. The interviewers began with a common set of questions and then probed their respondents with further questions following each response. Each interviewer then coded the transcripts thematically in order to draw up a matrix of codes, which were then reapplied to each transcript.

Findings

The Key Influences on Participants to Join the Programme

In order to evaluate the changes taking place at an individual level, we believed it important to establish a baseline for each interviewee by seeking to understand their values and beliefs prior to embarking on the programme, and how they accounted for these. We sought to discover, for example, what it was that they pinpointed in their biographies that had influenced them to engage politically or socially with the sustainability agenda, and whether and in what terms the participants described the influence of their family or educational background. We sought to understand the origins of their interest in the sustainability agenda, and how they made sense of this for themselves.

We found that a combination of early age, family, school, and university influences on participants had shaped their thinking and their environmental and social consciousness significantly. Many had early recollections of these early influences.

Family. Many respondents were brought up with an understanding or love of the countryside, often as a result of a rural upbringing and often reinforced by the influence of a family member. Most of the participants' parents were middle class, often teachers or academics, and many but not all had role modelled social or environmental awareness during their childhoods:

> I think my family did a huge amount, growing up on a farm and being out and about doing things . . . . I was surrounded by nature and natural environment and open space.

I've been very influenced by my family, my father particularly. He's a teacher. We went to Wales a lot as children. It was a safe, happy place for him. He talked about the land. It was quite romantic . . . . I don't think he was pushing me but he was passionate about it. That's what he talked about. I certainly don't think he'd be too thrilled if I became an accountant.

In terms of my interests in the environment and human rights, these had been throughout my childhood growing up . . . . I guess basically my parents were both very involved in their society and are both teachers—my sister and I were brought up to campaign for dolphins at about age six.

School. School experiences, and in particular the influence of specific teachers had also often fostered social and environmental awareness amongst the participants.

My advanced level geography teacher was very interesting. He may have been playing devil's advocate. I would have regular debates with him.

I was a keen biologist at school and had a very inspiring biology teacher who first got me into environmental issues. From there I went on to study biology at university, and at university I spent two summers in Cameroon trying to introduce bee-keeping.

University. These influences often led to specific university subject choices, the most common being geography, followed by science, engineering, and politics. The influences also often led to the decision to engage in political activities at university. For many, university represented the first opportunity to engage in political or environmental campaigning:

I did a degree in Environmental Engineering which looks at the problems of pollution especially in water and in air, and was about delivering healthy support systems to people.

Geography was my favourite subject at school and I did a geography degree up at Durham. It felt a natural step into the course. Geography is a very live subject —about people, the earth, and the planet. It wrapped me up and fired my imagination.

So I got involved with a student organisation and working a lot in Zimbabwe, that was my first real experience where I totally changed what I wanted to do from Marine Biology to International Development.

Other influences. Few of the participants mentioned political or world events as having been significant to them. Those that were mentioned were 9/11, the Gulf War, the emancipation of Nelson Mandela, and the influence of the "Live Aid" event in 1985:

> Things like the Gulf War—seeing the oil pluming across the Iraqi desert. That has left a very lasting mark on me.

> I'm just about old enough to remember Nelson Mandela being freed.

> I can remember the song [Live Aid] and being with my friend and listening to it in her kitchen, and thinking oh my God, what's going on? I must have been very young.

Political and environmental conventions such as Prague, Kyoto, and Montreal were also mentioned. Indeed, political, social, and environmental issues were a much greater influence on participants when they encountered them firsthand. Since most claimed to have comfortable, middle-class backgrounds, this begins to explain the huge influence of their gap year activities on their consciousness and engagement. Almost all the participants had taken a gap year. These activities, whether domestic work or overseas projects, stirred strong feelings in almost all our interviewees about injustice and inequity, environmental destruction, and the dominance of capitalism and global business:

> I had a year working for the Health and Development Department in Tamil Nadu. There were a lot of things I experienced which compounded my experience of sustainable development. I learned the impact of bad planning and bad decisions—the impact of political or financial decisions.

> When I was doing a gap year I worked on a conservation job in the Falklands for five months . . . you can see all the crap basically that washes up from the sea to beaches—flotsam and jetsam from all around the world that ends up in this pristine place.

What I did was to join the Prince's Trust Volunteer Scheme. That intense twelve weeks really sort of afforded me some perspective and a chance to look at what I wanted to do . . . that was a bit of a shock to the system but a very valuable one.

Programme Outcomes and Impact

Personal impact. The value of the programme was invariably constructed initially in terms of personal impact. This was wide-ranging, and included greater interpersonal awareness, self-confidence, self-belief, social skills, broader vision, and deeper understanding. A consistent message was that the programme represented excellent preparation for the world of work, a preparation that had not been provided by their undergraduate university education:

> The course allowed me to think of different ways of how to take the initiative. I think I'm more able to take an overview and to understand and be sympathetic to what people have to say. Through that you almost get automatically elevated to a very important member of the team. You become the hub for everyone. They kind of want to talk to you.

> If you want to talk to any individual or organisation or sector you really need to think about speaking in their language and speaking to them from a position that they will listen to.

> I was more able to understand the different ways people see and do things. That makes you more able to communicate with them more effectively.

This preparation for work and life also included the opportunity for graduates to learn firsthand what type of organisation they might want to join after completing their master's. Often being forced to undertake placements not of their choosing taught them a great deal and frequently changed their views and perspectives completely.

Learning from placements. Even those graduates who had been placed in organisations which were not their first choice had generally found them to be more useful than expected. As preparation for future career choices, the placements were also felt to have been essential for discovering what types of organisations suited them best and stimulated them. Often these discoveries were a revelation. They also spoke of the enormous value of learning about how organisations work, and the wider networks within the sustainable development arena:

I took a lot from all of the placements. The generic thing that you get from all of them is an awareness of organisational structure and how different sectors and segments are relating to each other.

I've been in BP now for two years and I probably learned 80 percent of how the organisation works during my one-month placement.

I learned that if you want to talk to any individual or organisation or sector you really need to think about speaking in their language and from a position that they will listen to.

Networks and networking skills. Almost without exception, the graduates volunteered that one of the most enduring legacies of the programme for them have been the networks that they developed during the programme, the people they had met and worked with, and the networking skills that they had learned and practised during the programme.

Some graduates said that they had found the emphasis on networking difficult to accept at the time, but had come to value the importance of this skill once they had embarked on their careers.

Some cohorts are still meeting at least once a year. Other industry-based groups of alumni graduates are also meeting for specific purposes. These networks are considered by many to be essential for their work, and by others as inspiring. There are, however, advantages and disadvantages of creating such tight-knit networks. For example, while the network is an excellent opportunity for peer support, there could be a lack of diversity, which may lead to the group being distanced from organisations they wish to influence.

I realised subsequently the extreme power of networking. It has helped me to develop my ideas, get funding, make friends, and just put everything together. It's just been pure networking. It's unbelievable.

I can go to a conference and confidently network around and come back with leads for new funding bids for the institute and that kind of thing . . . the experience from the programme has made me more rounded.

The programme gives you an invisible framework that I can then use. I've got a much different view of the world now. There is no way that I would have been accepted onto the PhD had I not been able to live and breathe the rhetoric of sustainable development and the kind of passion and understanding behind that.

Leadership skills. The majority of the participants in our study are not yet in senior roles in their organisations, but already many are finding ways to exert their influence. Many were able to point to specific learning taken from the leadership development component of the programme, and interestingly some had found that this learning had begun to make more sense since beginning their careers.

The messages taken from the programme varied from person to person, and the value was described in terms of what they have been able to use since leaving the programme. For one graduate it was about learning to question, for another it was about the Learning Cycle, another pointed to the art of self-reflection. Many remembered learning to give and receive feedback. Once again building self-confidence was a common theme, this time in relation to the skill of leadership. Some felt that they had not yet had the opportunity to put the learning into practice. Others echoed this, suggesting that since many graduates had joined the programme straight from university, the course may initially have assumed too much managerial and leadership experience.

> The thing that I regularly say when people ask me about the course is the only thing I genuinely think about every day is the stuff we did on the leadership development modules. In terms of being able to step back and achieve that critical distance within those kind of high pressured situations that's something that I've taken with me everywhere.

> I learnt a lot on the leadership course but I think I use it more now than I did then. . . . Act, reflect, and put into practice is a cycle I remember learning.

> I'm aware of the nature of the contributions I am making and I kind of try to step back a lot of the time and try to understand what is going on. I think that helps me to be effective.

> The leadership part of the programme totally changed the way in which I thought about making decisions, and the way I dealt with people in team situations.

Impact on the individual graduates' career success. One of the key aims of this research was to understand how the programme has affected the ability and success of individual graduates in their careers. The sections above have identified that personal skills, including networking and leadership ability, have been an important element of the programme in supporting them to be successful after the course. Many pointed to the lack of preparation for work offered by their undergraduate courses, and their gratitude to the programme for preparing them for organisational life. The level of influence of the graduates in their current jobs varied, but many were gratified that they were already playing a key role in their organisations and some were already able to influence policy:

> I can work in government and work at a relatively junior level and still influence policies, which is amazing.

> I'm sitting in the central environmental team of BP, which is the world's second biggest company. In that context I am quite a junior member but I have real influence on decisions. I have real impact and I'm working on some stuff which is potentially very exciting in terms of sustainability in the future.

> My work is spent facilitating and trying to move forward a partnership for oil and gas producers. All the big companies, BP, Shell, etc., are trying to put together a management system for an improved social and environmental impact assessment process. . . . Within BP we've now taken on board this process which has been quite good.

Social entrepreneurship. Most graduates are employed in NGOs, government, or industry. Almost all of those interviewed felt that they were contributing in some way to the sustainability agenda. One graduate demonstrated a very clear connection between her experience on the programme and her chosen vocation as a "social entrepreneur" as illustrated in her story below.

> We moved into our premises two hours ago! I've done all the development for it, and I did it unpaid for a year, part time. The aim is to make a profit, enough money to reinvest, nothing gets distributed to shareholders, but we do sell carpets at affordable prices to homeless people, and we do aim to cover our cost and make extra revenue to expand. We manufacture carpet slippers out of our leftovers. I'd like it to replicate in lots of other sites across the UK.

> I remember very clearly one lecturer mentioning the term social enterprise, and me going 'that's what I want to do. That's what I want to be.' Before that I always

assumed I was going into the civil service or politics. What I would like to do is to set up lots of social enterprises so this is just my first one.

The Graduates' Future Ambitions

Most graduates felt that the programme had cemented their involvement with sustainable development, but many were uncertain about how they would take their commitment forward in the future. Idealism was still strong, but this was tempered with a sense of realism and pragmatism that some felt they had gained from the programme. Some felt regret at having been confronted with the "realities" of the political and business world through the programme, which one graduate felt had "de-radicalised" him:

I feel tied into it [sustainable development] now. I don't think I could do something completely unrelated now.

I think that's really given me the confidence to go down a particular route and look for the opportunities within that route and explore it thoroughly. I don't think I'm a long way along the way yet. Who knows where the road will lead.

To some extent it has de-radicalised me. I'm not convinced that that's a very good thing. Before I did the course I wanted to work in NGOs and now I'm not sure if I could because I want to be able to work where I can actually see the wheels of power turning and make a difference and I think working in an NGO can possibly be very frustrating because you are banging on the doors from outside.

Discussion

This paper has focused on the benefits of a work-based sustainable development master's programme for the participants in terms of their ability to operate success-fully in their chosen work and make a contribution to the sustainable development agenda. Key insights into what has influenced students to join the programme have been highlighted. This research has found that the programme has impacted on students in three key areas: personal development, networking, and leadership skills.

With regard to personal development the findings show evidence of increased self-confidence, improved social and political skills, adaptability, and a wider and deeper understanding of organisations and the way that graduates function in them. In addition, programme graduates saw the networks they developed within the programme, and their enhanced networking skills, as a vital benefit. Even those who resisted the importance of networking during the programme agreed that this skill was one of the most important for progressing the sustainable development agenda through their work. Most of the graduates spoke warmly of the network of programme alumni, and in particular the closeness of the support of the others in their own year.

> ❝ **THE FINDINGS SHOW EVIDENCE OF INCREASED SELF-CONFIDENCE, IMPROVED SOCIAL AND POLITICAL SKILLS, ADAPTABILITY, AND A WIDER AND DEEPER UNDERSTANDING OF ORGANISATIONS.** ❞

Not all graduates had accepted the relevance of developing leadership skills at the time, but many said they now draw extensively on the learning they took from the leadership modules. Many still use some of the ideas from this module in their work. The most often cited ideas were the importance of stepping back and reflecting to achieve a critical distance, giving and receiving feedback, understanding one's strengths and areas for development, adopting a cycle of practice and reflection, and the importance of learning self-control. A survey of alumni attending the annual weekend at the Leadership Trust asked, "What achievements are you most proud of?" and "How did the course help you achieve these?" The results confirmed the findings above and in addition showed that the alumni rated the ability to inspire and motivate others.

Three areas therefore emerged as having an impact on students: leadership development, work experience, and networking. Firstly, leadership development based on experiential learning had an impact on both self-development (self-confidence and self-awareness) of individuals and the development of their relationship building skills (building respect and trust). Secondly, the experience gained in differing sectors of society through work-based learning impacted on the ability of graduates to have influence within and across organisations. This was owing to the empathy gained from differing views and opinions regarding sustainable development from differing sectors. The alumni survey in 2006 also showed that a deeper theoretical understanding of sustainable development was also an important component of course learning. This sound intellectual grounding complemented by confidence and awareness of cultures in different sectors was identified as a vital combination.

The alumni survey identified that the achievements the alumni were most proud of were setting up new businesses, developing new tools and techniques, and establishing new projects. It is noticeable that they are proud of new initiatives, indicating that the ability to spot opportunities and to innovate were important skills that they developed. These skills were not explicitly identified as something the course gave them, but they did recognise that the course emphasis on practical implementation and in particular the big group project were important.

Furthermore, the graduates felt they were better prepared for the world of work as a result of the programme. This was centred on a greater ability to understand what they did and did not want to do after the course and they felt that they had developed skills that were transferable due to the different experiences in different sectors. The research also found that a significant factor impacting upon student learning occurred when a student went on a placement initially not preferred by the student.

> ## " THREE AREAS EMERGED AS HAVING AN IMPACT ON STUDENTS: LEADERSHIP DEVELOPMENT, WORK EXPERIENCE, AND NETWORKING. "

While the findings herein support Burgoyne's (2006) proposition that there are three outcomes from leadership development activities (confidence, pause for reflection, and networking), this research provides evidence of deeper insights into these propositions. For example, the findings of this research provide evidence to support the suggestion that leadership development appears to increase confidence. This research, however, appears to be uncovering a myriad of constitutive constructs that include such concepts as self-awareness and self-control.

This research also provides evidence to support the process of leadership development that includes work-based learning, theory, and social interaction highlighted earlier (Bentley & Turnbull, 2005) and the model of change for sustainable development that includes awareness, agency, and association (Ballard, 2005). The findings of this research suggest that the programme responds appropriately to the call for leadership of sustainable development issues (c.f. Bernhut, 2004; Giampalmi, 2004; Reid et al., 2002) using this methodology.

The programme goes further, however, by stressing the importance of the leadership context in terms of ensuring that leaders that are being developed are knowledgeable about relationships within and between functions in and around organisations (Giampalmi, 2004). Our findings suggest that placements, in particular, hold the key to the development of contextually sensitive leadership ability. This is important given the argument that being proactive with respect to sustainable development may mean different things in different organisational contexts (Vredenburg & Westley, 1999). This paper provides supporting evidence for this argument and evidence that the programme develops leaders able to confront this type of complexity.

Recommendations for Further Research

It is clear that the programme has had significant impact at the level of the individuals, their career paths, and their influence in their roles. It is too early to evaluate the impact on organisations, society, and the sustainability agenda as most of the graduates are very early in their careers. A further study of graduate impact in five years is recommended. At this point it will become clear what impact they have had on the bigger sustainability agenda and how the graduates' careers have progressed.

Furthermore, this research project has been restricted to focusing on the participants themselves and their biographical accounts. It is recognised that this is not the complete picture, and that an understanding of their progress and leadership may be more fully gauged by extending the survey to work colleagues in their current organisations. This was beyond the scope of the current project, but this may be a logical next step. We also recommend that the next phase of research into the impact and outcomes of the programme will be at the level of the organisation(s) in which the graduates work or have worked. Having completed these two levels of analysis, the final level to be evaluated over the longer term will then be impact on communities/society.

Conclusions

This paper concludes that the programme is having an impact on its graduates and how they interact in organisations and sectors based on the sustainability agenda. This research provides evidence to support the process of leadership development that includes work-based learning, theory, and social interaction highlighted earlier and the model of change for sustainable development that includes awareness, agency, and association. The findings of this research suggest that the master's programme responds positively to the call for leadership of sustainable development issues using the three core elements highlighted earlier in the paper. The programme goes further, however, by ensuring that leaders that are being developed are knowledgeable about relationships within and between functions in and around organisations. It seems placements, in particular, hold the key to the development of contextually sensitive leadership ability.

REFERENCES

Azapagic, A. (2003). Systems approach to corporate sustainability: A general management framework. *Trans IchemE, 81*(Part B), 303–316.

Ballard, D. (2005). Using learning processes to promote change for sustainable development. *Action Research, 3*(2), 135–156.

Bentley, J., & Turnbull, S. (2005). Stimulating leadership—The ten key triggers of leadership development. In R. W. T. Gill (Ed.), *Leadership under the microscope* (pp. 35–53). Ross-on-Wye, Herefordshire, UK: The Leadership Trust Foundation.

Bernhut, S. (2004, March/April). Sumantra Ghoshal on leadership, management and good governance. *Ivey Business Journal*, pp. 1–4.

Burgoyne, J. G. (2006). *Design, facilitation, contextualisation and evaluation of learning for leadership development.* Paper presented at the University of Exeter, Centre for Leadership Studies Lent Seminar Series, 2nd February.

Coopey, J. (2003). Sustainable development and environmental management: The performance of UK business schools. *Management Learning, 34*(1), 5–26.

Edwards, G. P., & Gill, R. W. T. (2005). *Leadership cluster initiative evaluation report.* Research Report (Research Centre for Leadership Studies, The Leadership Trust Foundation, Ross-on-Wye, Herefordshire, UK).

Edwards, G. P., & Turnbull, S. (2005). Evaluating the impact of leadership development in a regional sports partnership: A case study. In R. W. T. Gill (Ed.), *Leadership under the microscope* (pp. 83–100). Ross-on-Wye, Herefordshire, UK: The Leadership Trust Foundation.

Forum for the Future. (2007). Retrieved from http://www.forumforthefuture.org.uk

Giampalmi, J. (2004, October/November). Leading chaos, paradox and dysfunctionality in sustainable development. *Executive Speeches*, pp. 6–13.

Gill, R. W. T., & Edwards, G. P. (2003). *Leadership development case study: An evaluation of the impact of the Leadership Trust's course, 'Leadership in Management,' in a multinational organisation.* Working paper No. LT-RG-03-24. (Research Centre for Leadership Studies, The Leadership Trust Foundation, Ross-on-Wye, Herefordshire, UK).

Johnson, D., & Beloff, B. (1998, Spring). Educating future leaders for a sustainable path. *Environmental Quality Management*, pp. 31–39.

W. K. Kellogg Foundation. (1998). *Evaluation handbook.* Retrieved July 6, 2000, from http://www.wkkf.org/pubs/Pub770.pdf

W. K. Kellogg Foundation. (2002). *Evaluating outcomes and impacts: A scan of 55 leadership development programmes.* Available from http://www.wkkf.org

Marzano, R. J. (1993). Lessons from the field about outcomes-based performance assessment. *Educational Leadership, 51*(6), 44–50.

Reid, A., Scott, W., & Gough, S. (2002). Education and sustainable development in the UK: An exploration of progress since Rio. *Geography, 87*(3), 247–255.

Schalock, R. L. (2001). *Outcomes-based evaluation.* London: Kluwer Academic/Plenum Publishers.

Shinn, S. (2005, July/August). Sustainability at the core. *BizEd*, pp. 30–38.

Stake, R. (1967). The countenance of educational evaluation. *Teachers College Record, 68*(7), 523–540.

Turnbull, S., & Edwards, G. P. (2005). Developing leaders for organisational change in a new university. In R. W. T. Gill (Ed.), *Leadership under the microscope* (pp. 69–82). Ross-on-Wye, Herefordshire, UK: The Leadership Trust Foundation.

Vredenburg, H., & Westley, F. (1999). Sustainable development leadership in three contexts: Managing for global competitiveness. *Journal of Business Administration and Policy Analysis, 27*, 239–260.

Welford, R., & Ytterhus, B. (2004). Sustainable development and tourism destination management: A case study of the Lillehammer region, Norway. *International Journal of Sustainable Development and World Ecology, 11*, 410–422.

Zimmerman-Oster, K., & Burkhardt, J. C. (1999). Leadership in the making: A comprehensive examination of the impact of leadership development programs on students. *The Journal of Leadership Studies, 6*(3/4), 51–65.

DR. GARETH EDWARDS is a Senior Researcher in the Centre for Applied Leadership Research at the Leadership Trust Foundation in the UK and is a Visiting Research Fellow at the University of Portsmouth Business School, also in the UK. Gareth is a Chartered Psychologist and serves as a Course Director and tutor on the courses run by The Leadership Trust and works on programme design, diagnosis, and evaluation.

SHARON TURNBULL is Director of the Centre for Applied Leadership Research. She is also Visiting Professor at Gloucestershire University, Senior Visiting Research Fellow at Lancaster University Management School, Fellow at Durham Business School, and a Chartered Fellow of the Chartered Institute of Personnel and Development. Sharon has researched, published, taught, and consulted to organisations in the field of organisational culture and change, and has a background in human resource development.

DAVID STEPHENS is Professor of International Education at the University of Brighton. He has worked extensively in Northern and Southern universities in the UK on the quality of basic education and the relationship between culture and educational development. From 2004–2005 he was head of master's programmes at Forum for the Future.

DR. ANDY JOHNSTON is Principal Sustainability Advisor at Forum for the Future. He has been Course Director for the master's in Leadership for Sustainable Development for five years and is also responsible for promoting leadership in the UK public sector. Previously he was a lecturer at the University of Hertfordshire in the UK.

Leading into a Sustainable Future: The Current Challenge

By Benjamin Redekop

AS THE EARTH'S POPULATION GROWS EVER LARGER AND ENVIRON-mental degradation continues apace, it is becoming increasingly clear that we need to learn to live in a more sustainable fashion, or else risk the collapse of existing social, political, and ecological systems (Diamond, 2005; Meadows, Randers, & Meadows, 2004). This is a challenge for leadership—perhaps the greatest single leadership challenge of this and coming generations. Given the ravages of Hurricane Katrina and the looming spectre of global warming, it was apt that Machiavelli used the image of a flood to warn princes against the dangers of shortsightedness. It is easy for leaders to be lulled into complacency, Machiavelli warned, when things are going well, but time and circumstance (*fortuna*) are such that those who do not adequately prepare for the future by building dikes are likely to be swept away when the floodwaters rise (Machiavelli, 1513/1983, pp. 130–131).

Changing circumstances are forcing us to reconsider the very nature of leadership. I would like to suggest that *sustainability* is no longer an optional element of leadership, if it ever was, but a central task.[1] If the great leadership challenges of the past involved bringing into being such things as liberty, equality, national unity, and prosperity, the current and future task may well be to simply *sustain* the existing world system, while still seeking to raise up those who have yet to benefit from modernity. Although no one wants to discount the advances of past political, social, and economic movements and the continued potential for realizing their gains throughout the world, it is entirely possible that the plight of many of the world's poor will actually get worse—think of low-lying coastal areas in South Asia—if environmental sustainability is not soon achieved (Doyle, 2007; Fogarty, 2004; IPCC, 2007; Stern, 2006). Highly respected scientists like James Hansen, Director of the NASA Goddard Institute for Space Studies, are now passionately calling for leadership on the climate change issue in particular (Hansen, 2006). However, achieving a state of lasting global equilibrium[2] is a leadership challenge that will entail unprecedented attention to the future consequences of present actions.

Leadership and the Future

Leadership is enacted in both space and time. It is most often conceived in spatial terms: the leader is the person physically "out in front" of the group; they take us some*where*—to a place that we want to go. But leadership equally involves being out in front *in time*. There must be some sense of where we are going and how we are going to get there, and it is an act of leadership to have this knowledge and convey it convincingly to one's constituents. Leadership involves, among other things, setting future goals and helping others to meet them.

 WE NEED TO LEARN TO LIVE IN A MORE SUSTAINABLE FASHION, OR ELSE RISK THE COLLAPSE OF EXISTING SOCIAL, POLITICAL, AND ECOLOGICAL SYSTEMS. "

Thus James MacGregor Burns, in his classic work on *Leadership*, states: "I define leadership as the leaders inducing followers to act for certain goals that represent the values and the motivations . . . of both leaders and followers" (Burns, 1978, p. 19; see also Bass, 1990, pp. 14–16; Northouse, 2007, p. 3). Robert Greenleaf's servant leader is more explicitly visionary than Burns's transforming leader; it is not enough to help followers reach their goals, leaders must also have a prophetic vision of the future state into which followers are being led: "Foresight is the 'lead' that the leader has. Once leaders lose this lead and events start to force their hand, they are leaders in name only" (Greenleaf, 2002, p. 40). In Winston and Patterson's (2006) integrative definition of leadership, drawn from a broad survey of the leadership literature, future orientation plays a central role: "The leader achieves . . . influence by humbly conveying a prophetic vision of the future in clear terms that resonates with the follower(s) beliefs and values in such a way that the follower(s) can understand and interpret the future into present-time actions steps" (p. 7).

Bolman and Deal assert that "Vision is the only characteristic of effective leadership that is universal" (as cited in Harter, 2006, p. 21). The degree of future orientation can be seen as one of the key distinctions between leaders and managers— the higher the organizational position, the greater the emphasis on future orientation (Bass, 1990, pp. 404–406; Kouzes & Posner, 2002, pp. 28–29). This distinction has the merit of also being congruent with everyday language: "to manage" connotes activity in the here-and-now, while "to lead" suggests forward motion in both space and time.

Thus whatever the other many and varied qualities of leadership, vision and future orientation go to the heart of what is generally understood by the term. What this means in practice, however, has often been left vague, undeveloped, or very narrowly focused, particularly in business books on leadership. Mainstream works on business leadership that make future orientation a central theme typically contain neither a substantive analysis of the psychology of future orientation, nor a sense of the larger systemic constraints on future activities that must be taken into account by leaders. The physical environment, the ultimate constraint on business, is entirely ignored (e.g., Corbin, 2000; Essex & Kusy, 1999; James, 1996). Although Kouzes and Posner (2002) mention the need for visionary leaders to care for something larger than themselves, they suggest that envisioning the future is merely a process of "discovering [your own] themes . . . . Finding your vision, like finding your voice, is a process of self-exploration and self-creation. It's an intuitive, emotional process. There's often no logic to it" (p. 115).

66 CHANGING CIRCUMSTANCES ARE FORCING US TO RECONSIDER THE VERY NATURE OF LEADERSHIP. 99

Even prominent works that claim to be "the definitive text" on future leadership, such as *The Leader of the Future* (Hesselbein, Goldsmith, & Beckhard, 1996), contain little substantive reflection on the larger systemic constraints on future activity. To be fair, the recently updated edition of this text, titled *The Leader of the Future 2* (Hesselbein & Goldsmith, 2006), is somewhat improved on this score—Peter Senge's chapter discusses the need for leaders to be involved in systemic change in the face of global constraints, including the constraints posed by the natural environment and global warming (Senge, 2006). In the same collection, Ronald Heifetz's discussion of leadership as a response to "adaptive challenges" is an important contribution to understanding leadership as a forward-looking response to deep and difficult challenges, and he even goes to the brink of the current environmental abyss, suggesting that "Some realities threaten not only a set of values beyond survival but also the very existence of a society if these realities are not discovered and met early on." Yet although environmental problems like global warming are obviously supreme examples of adaptive challenges, Heifetz seems unwilling to explicitly draw that conclusion, or to identify himself with the "many environmentalists [who believe] our focus on the production of wealth rather than coexistence with nature has led us to neglect fragile factors in our ecosystem" (Heifetz, 2006, pp. 82–83).

Well-informed individuals who understand how science works no longer have any reason to doubt that we are facing, now and over the coming generations, a serious environmental crisis with a variety of dimensions and causes. Many environmental problems are well-known, obvious, and getting worse (see, for example, the exhaustive list in Diamond, 2005, pp. 486–496). Other problems, like climate change, have only recently come into focus, as "an overwhelming scientific consensus" (Hansen, 2006, p. 11) has emerged that human beings are causing significant changes in the global climate system that, if not addressed, will result in a host of negative outcomes, not least of which is a severe, long-term, negative economic impact (IPCC, 2007, 2007a; Joint Science Academies Statement, 2005; Stern, 2006). The challenge presented by climate change is so daunting that it merits urgent attention. Current estimates are that global greenhouse gas emissions are going to need to be reduced 80 percent below current levels by 2050 (which means developed nations need to reduce their emissions by 95 percent) if catastrophic warming is to be avoided—i.e., to keep the increase over the current average temperature to "only" 2 degrees Celsius by 2100 (Doyle, 2007a). The various scenarios projected in the Intergovernmental Panel on Climate Change Fourth Assessment predict a 1.8 to 4.0 degree Celsius temperature rise by century's end, with an average "best estimate" of 2.8 degrees Celsius (IPCC, 2007a, p. 13). A change of that magnitude is enough to produce what NASA climate scientist James Hansen calls "a transformed planet" (Hansen, 2006, p. 4), with serious social, economic, and environmental impacts, most of them negative.

> **" " *SUSTAINABILITY* IS NO LONGER AN OPTIONAL ELEMENT OF LEADERSHIP. " "**

Meanwhile, coal-fired power-generating stations have been brought online worldwide at the rate of two per week over the past five years, and plans are being made "to add enough coal-fired capacity in the next five years to create an extra 1.2 billion tons of CO_2 per year" (Clayton, 2007). Technological solutions like carbon sequestration are urgently needed, but the scope of the challenge is so great that it seems highly unlikely that technical innovations alone will solve the problem, which appears already to have reached a crucial "tipping point" (Hansen, 2006, p. 10; Zabarenko, 2006). Rapid and far-reaching economic, social, political, and lifestyle changes will clearly need to occur if a truly sustainable world system is to be achieved, and this is a challenge that reaches beyond science and technology to leadership.

The deficit in taking a serious, long-term perspective on the future in the field of leadership studies reflects both the field's orientation toward the limited time horizons of Anglo/U.S. capitalism, and the general worldview of the first Industrial Revolution, in which the future was seen to be limitless and constraints on economic and industrial activity were either ignored (as in the case of air and water pollution) or strongly opposed (as in the emergence of organized labor). We are now becoming increasingly aware of the way in which modern industry has been built on the externalization of costs: early on the costs were more social and ethical—slavery and child labor were bound up with early industrialization (Mathias, 1969; Williams, 1961), but increasingly the environmental costs of industry have taken center stage. The tendency among students of American business leadership to ignore or discount the larger social and environmental contexts in which leadership occurs is simply a reflection of some of the main tenets of American capitalism, as well as the lineaments of the American dream, which stresses the idea that human beings (and by extension, leaders) are free agents who can succeed at whatever they wish to do, if only they work hard enough. Critics have argued for some time that placing too much emphasis on leaders as free agents ignores the fact that "the leader is embedded in a social system, which constrains behavior" (Pfeffer, 1977, p. 107). Thirty years later, we must add that leaders are also embedded in a global *environmental* system that also represents a serious constraint on behavior.

❝   LEADERSHIP INVOLVES BEING OUT IN FRONT   ❞
IN TIME.

I do not wish to imply that no good work is being done that confronts the need for long-term, sustainable leadership, whether in business, politics, or the nonprofit sector, or that the heroic figure of the leader-as-free-agent is unchallenged in the field—many new approaches have begun to take a much broader look at leadership. It is beyond the scope of this chapter to survey current thinking in the field that holds promise for addressing environmental problems. Nor do I wish to suggest that no actual leadership is being shown on the issue in the North American context. Numerous groups and individuals are heroically tackling the problem—including political figures like Al Gore, businessmen like Ray Anderson, and scientists like David Suzuki and James Hansen, to name but a few. Anderson stands out as a truly visionary business leader who has thought through the implications of the current environmental crisis and shown how businesses can combine environmental sustainability with profitability (Anderson, 1998). In the field of leadership studies, recent works by Crosby (1999), Avery (2005), and Hargreaves and Fink (2006) directly address sustainable leadership in the public sector, business, and education, respectively, and there are doubtless more works in progress on the topic. Nevertheless, it is clear that we are at the beginning of a very long road to environmental sustainability, and we have only begun to analyze the problem from the point of view of the demands that will be placed on leaders (whether as individuals or collectivities). A recent survey of the literature on public-sector leadership, for example, barely mentions the natural environment as an area of concern for leaders (Kellerman & Webster, 2001).

Time Orientation and the Challenge of the Future

Perhaps one of the biggest challenges that leaders will encounter is the fact that the negative effects of present behaviors will not be fully felt for decades: making the connection between individual behaviors and global outcomes challenges moral faculties that were evolved in small hunter-gatherer communities. Moral concern weakens with distance—we do not come naturally equipped to care very much about what happens to people, plants, and animals on the other side of the continent, much less on the other side of the planet (Hauser, 2006). And temporally the situation is similar. As Reading (2004) puts it, "It is difficult enough to go without something in order to enhance our own future well-being, let alone do it to benefit unknown generations that have yet to come" (p. 171).

Avoiding global environmental catastrophe and achieving sustainability is thus an enormous challenge not least because doing so entails resolving a conflict between immediate individual wants and long-term collective good. Acting as self-interested individuals, we tend to exploit common resources, especially if the benefits are clear and immediate and the costs are diffuse and located far in the future. Garrett Hardin called this the "tragedy of the commons" (Hardin, 1968), while others refer to it as a "social dilemma" (Joireman, 2005). As Hardin suggested, there is no problem so long as populations are limited and resources are plentiful. But at some point unlimited population growth and resource depletion entail the general collapse of a finite system, which hurts everyone. In order to avoid this tragic outcome, individuals need to align their behavior with the long-term best interests of the community and, indeed, biosphere. Doing so may sound simple, but it is enormously difficult to achieve, and represents a real leadership challenge.

Research into time orientation and future-oriented behavior helps us to appreciate the human dimensions of the challenge and can furnish insights to leaders. In historical terms, modernity brought with it an unprecedented future orientation. In contrast to the cyclical patterns which characterize most traditional, pre-literate, and non-entrepreneurial cultures, a widely shared linear time orientation arose in the early modern period, in tandem with the emergence of modern science and technology, capitalism, democratic politics, and industry. During the eighteenth-century Enlightenment the idea that history was progressive and that conditions were improving for "man" at large became pervasive—the future began to look very bright indeed, at least for those in a position to reflect on the matter. For the first time in history it became thinkable that new knowledge was better than old knowledge, and that moderns were advancing beyond the achievements of the ancients. "Improvement" became a theme of enlighteners and educators throughout Europe and America. The Industrial Revolution, built as it was on technological advancement and the rationalization of production processes, helped to secure the notion that time is linear, progressive, and governable, and that the future is not only bright but can be predicted and controlled in ways that go far beyond the traditional methods of astrology, divination, and reliance on prophets and soothsayers. During subsequent centuries "progress" became a guiding theme of Western culture.[3]

> **" WE HAVE ONLY BEGUN TO ANALYZE THE PROBLEM "
> OF SUSTAINABILITY FROM THE POINT OF VIEW OF
> THE DEMANDS THAT WILL BE PLACED ON LEADERS.**

Yet as Reading (2004) suggests, "There is [now] a growing apprehension about the future. As people begin to realize that nature often exacts a price for the gains that science and technology bring, progress is no longer seen as an unalloyed blessing. Threats of environmental or nuclear disaster make the future seem less hospitable than it once did" (p. 126). Nowotny (1994) puts the matter this way: "Progress itself, it may be said, has aged. In the ecological sphere, the repercussions are the most dramatic, because here linearity—the continuous pushing out on a continuum temporally directed towards the future—has most drastically and most lastingly turned out to be an unfounded hope" (p. 49). The buildup of ecological waste (including atmospheric CO_2) is one of the products of time that weighs on the present and belies the modern conception of the future as a limitless repository of all our hopes and dreams—but not our waste.

Whatever the large-scale historical and cultural changes in conceptions of the future, scholars are gaining increasing insight into the psychology of future orientation. Joireman, Strathman, and Balliet (2006) have proposed an integrative model of a personality variable called Consideration of Future Consequences (CFC). According to this research, individuals high in CFC tend to be more conscientious, academically successful, able to delay gratification and avoid unhealthy habits, and less impulsive and hedonistic. They also tend to be more interested and involved in pro-environmental behaviors (Joireman, 2005; Joireman et al., 2006). People low in CFC tend to focus on the immediate consequences of behaviors; engage in riskier behaviors; and are higher in present hedonism, fatalism, depression, and drug use, among other things. Those high in CFC are apparently better able to connect present behaviors with future consequences than those lower in CFC, and they act accordingly. The implication for leadership is the need to identify and empower individuals high in CFC, and help individuals low in CFC to recognize and act on those connections in a meaningful and enduring fashion. Research shows that in order to do so, leaders will need to be able to make clear to people low in CFC how cooperating with proposed solutions to environmental problems will benefit them in *both* the short and long term (Joireman, 2005, pp. 298–299).

Leaders must be able to induce positive emotional states if constituents are to engage in future-oriented behaviors, since people tend to emphasize short-term outcomes when they are in a negative emotional state. Hope is a positive emotion that allows us to delay present satisfactions for future rewards, and as such must be nurtured if people are to be convinced to act in a future-oriented manner. When people become less hopeful about the future, they typically become more short-sighted, cynical, and self-centered (Cottle & Klineberg, 1974; Joireman et al., 2006; Reading, 2004). As Reading notes, "Hope gives us a vision that things can be better . . . an expectation that some desired goal can be attained. It has been the driving force behind all of humanity's great achievements through the ages . . . . Future-oriented behavior is the behavioral signal of hope" (2004, pp. 3–5). Hopeful behaviors are augmented by clearly articulated, achievable goals that are congruent with an individual's value system (Snyder, Rand, & Ritschel, 2006). From this perspective, then, "one of the main tasks of leadership is to articulate a credible vision of the future that embodies the hopes and aspirations of their followers . . . . Successful leaders raise a group's morale and bolster its members' hopes of achieving their desired goals" (Reading, 2004, p. 143).

In a similar vein, even though there is some utility in raising awareness of future threats, a strong correlation has been found to exist between Future Anxiety (FA) and negative expectations of solutions to global problems, threats, and dangers, with concomitant (negative) behaviors (Zaleski, 2005, pp. 133–134). Leaders must therefore engage in a delicate balancing act, identifying threats while communicating optimism about the chances of countering them. Complicating the issue, however, are two related findings. One is that "Cooperation in social dilemmas declines as the size of the resource becomes more uncertain" (Joireman, 2005, p. 298). We cooperate less in solving resource problems if we are unsure just how limited the resource is—maybe the problem is not so pressing after all! Secondly, "We are more frequently cooperative as the endpoint of the interaction seems ever-farther away" (Parks & Posey, 2005, p. 238). Cooperation, in other words, is heightened if we are all convinced that this is a long-term issue that will not be solved tomorrow (by someone else's sacrifice). Taken together, these findings suggest that too much optimism about the extent of available resources and the probability of immediate success can result in backsliding and exacerbation of the problem. If too much FA is counterproductive, so is too little.

Further compounding the problem, the environmental goal to be reached is what psychologists call an "avoidance goal," rather than a more positive "approach goal" (Snyder et al., 2006). Environmental collapse is something to be avoided; we are not talking about the discovery of El Dorado or Shangri-la, we are just hoping to hold onto what we have. The problem with avoidance goals is that they often do not have a clear endpoint. Consequently, "Such goal pursuits do not result in positive emotions nor in the general sense of well-being that are the sequelae of approach goals" (Snyder et al., 2006, p. 109). Leaders will need to re-frame the avoidance goal of environmental collapse into a more positive approach goal or, better yet, series of goals that can be celebrated as they are met.

A loss of hope, as often happens among the poor and indigent, is a likely cause of short-term behaviors (Cottle & Klineberg, 1974; Edwards, 2002), and this fact raises the issue of economic inequality: is it possible to expect future-oriented behavior from people hardly able to survive? Cottle and Klineberg (1974) argue that fatalism among the poor is most likely a result of bad or hopeless living conditions, not "any psychological inability to imagine a different future as a personal possibility" (p. 183). If the health of the planet requires that all human beings engage in environmentally sensitive behaviors, then is it not a requirement of sustainability that the poor be raised up to a level of prosperity that allows them to be more future oriented? It is well-known that wealth and prosperity are correlated with CFC (Cottle & Klineberg, 1974; Friedman, 1990; Joireman et al., 2006). It is an open question whether CFC causes wealth and success, whether wealth and success cause CFC, or some combination of the two. But clearly it is much easier to be future-oriented when one is not simply struggling to survive. The bottom line is that the wealthy—many of us in North America, for example—are in a better position to be future-oriented than poor nations, and thus we have a responsibility to lead the way on sustainability. To claim that we cannot act to curb greenhouse gas emissions until developing nations do the same, especially given the fact that we are one of the main parties responsible for the existing problem, is a clear abdication of leadership and, indeed, responsibility.

Conclusion: The Sustainable Leader as Storyteller and Image-Maker

My aim in this chapter has been to explore what it means to say that leadership involves conveying a prophetic vision of the future, in a world of environmental constraints and diminishing natural resources. I have come at the issue of sustainable leadership from the perspective of future orientation; however, achieving sustainability is a complex, multifaceted leadership challenge that requires study and analysis from numerous angles, and is therefore an important and promising topic for future research. Crosby (1999) has provided one of the most substantive recent treatments of the specific challenges and techniques of global public-sector leadership, while Avery (2005) provides an excellent starting-point for further thinking about sustainable business leadership. And the work of Peter Senge and colleagues (e.g., Senge et al., 2007) is required reading for anyone interested in a comprehensive, systemic analysis of collaborative organizational responses to the problem.

A particularly intriguing approach to the challenge of inspiring change in the direction of sustainability is to view leaders as image-makers and storytellers. As Harter (2006) suggests, leaders engage followers in a mutual process of shaping mental images of reality. "Leadership is the process by which one person exposes and replaces the fallacy of misplaced concreteness, enabling others to gain separation from their preexisting mental constructs—of themselves, each other, their social context, and possible futures—so that we might all see things anew, nearer in fact to the reality where ultimately we wish to flourish" (p. 25).

Stephen Denning, in *The Leader's Guide to Storytelling* (2005), provides an insightful analysis of one important way in which images are enacted in human minds—through stories and other narrative forms. Literary theorists, philosophers, and psychologists have long explored the role of narrative and rhetoric in shaping human perceptions of reality. Denning draws on this research to offer a practical, accessible guide to storytelling as an art of persuasion relevant to business (and other) leaders. Denning emphasizes the degree to which storytelling is a key component of human behavior—and leadership—and the ways in which leaders can most effectively inspire their constituents through stories, including what he calls the "springboard" story—a story of a past challenge that was overcome which can be applied, in the minds of listeners, to their own challenges.

Particularly pertinent to the present discussion is Denning's insistence that future stories must not be too specific, since particular outcomes are hard to predict and hence are easily discredited. "An inherent characteristic of a successful speech about the future is likely to be the lack of specificity and the evocativeness of the language" (Denning, 2005, p. 233). Leaders must leave it up to followers to put flesh and blood on their future visions: this allows followers to make the story their own, while allowing the vision to be adapted to the twists and turns of history as it unfolds. Crosby (1999) furthermore suggests that a good future story reflects an image of their best selves back to an audience, while giving individuals a sense of their connection to a larger community of interest and concern (p. 128). In this and other ways—many yet to be conceived—we can begin to understand how we as leaders and followers can help bring into being a world that lasts.

NOTES

1. See note 2 for a discussion of what I mean by "sustainability." One of Machiavelli's underlying assumptions, which is evident throughout *The Prince*, is that the greatest rulers and states are those that *endure* (see, for example, Machiavelli, 1513/1983, p. 79). I owe this insight to Michael Harvey, who also made a number of other helpful comments and suggestions that have strengthened the chapter.

2. This is the term used by Meadows et al. (1972, pp. 156–184) that helps to clarify what I mean by "sustainable." As I am using the term, a sustainable practice or mode of living is one that endures beyond the span of a few human lifetimes without causing severe disruption to the larger natural system of which it is a part, and is "capable of satisfying the basic material requirements of its people" (Meadows et al., 1972, p. 158). The ultimate point of reference for sustainability is the expanse of geologic time, against which human civilization is thus far barely a speck.

3. Many historical and anthropological sources could be cited here, but these developments are so well known that I will limit myself to mentioning a few synthetic works on time orientation: Bell, 1997; Cottle & Klineberg, 1974; Nowotny, 1994; Reading, 2004. Suffice it to say that these are broad generalizations to which there are numerous exceptions, and which can be qualified in various ways.

REFERENCES

Anderson, R. (1998). *Mid-course correction: Toward a sustainable enterprise—the Interface model.* White River Junction, VT: Chelsea Green Publishing Company.

Avery, G. (2005). *Leadership for sustainable futures: Achieving success in a competitive world.* Cheltenham, UK: Edward Elgar Publishing.

Bass, B. (1990). *Bass & Stogdill's handbook of leadership: Theory, research, and managerial applications.* New York: The Free Press.

Bell, W. (1997). *Foundations of future studies: Human science for a new era.* New Brunswick, NJ: Transaction Publishers.

Burns, J. (1978). *Leadership.* New York: Harper Perennial.

Clayton, M. (2007, March 22). Global boom in coal power—and emissions. *The Christian Science Monitor.* Retrieved from http://www.csmonitor.com/2007/0322/p01s04-wogi.htm

Corbin, C. (2000). *Great leaders see the future first: Taking your organization to the top in five revolutionary steps.* Chicago: Dearborn.

Cottle, T., & Klineberg, S. (1974). *The present of things future.* New York: The Free Press.

Crosby, B. (1999). *Leadership for global citizenship: Building transnational community.* Thousand Oaks, CA: Sage Publications.

Denning, S. (2005). *The leader's guide to storytelling.* San Francisco: Jossey-Bass.

Diamond, J. (2005). *Collapse: How societies choose to fail or succeed.* New York: Viking.

Doyle, A. (2007, March 28). One in 10 at risk from rising seas, storms: Study. *Reuters.* Retrieved from http://www.reuters.com/article/ScienceNews/idUSL2714227620070328

Doyle, A. (2007a, April 19). World needs to axe greenhouse gases by 80 pct: Report. *Reuters.* Retrieved from http://www.reuters.com/article/idUSL194440620070419

Edwards, A. J. (2002). *A psychology of time orientation: Time awareness across life stages and in dementia.* Westport, CT: Praeger.

Essex, L., & Kusy, M. (1999). *Fast-forward leadership: How to exchange outmoded leadership practices for forward-looking leadership today*. London: Pearson Education Limited.

Fogarty, D. (2004). Asia faces living nightmare from climate change. *Reuters*. Retrieved from http://www.unep.org/cpi/briefs/Brief26Nov04.doc

Friedman, W. (1990). *About time: Inventing the fourth dimension*. Cambridge, MA: MIT.

Greenleaf, R. (2002). *Servant leadership: A journey into the nature of legitimate power and greatness*. New York: Paulist Press.

Hansen, J. (2006). The threat to the planet. *The New York Review of Books*. Retrieved from http://www.nybooks.com/articles/19131

Hardin, G. (1968). The tragedy of the commons. *Science, 162*(3859), 1243–1248.

Hargreaves, A., & Fink, D. (2006). *Sustainable leadership*. San Francisco: Jossey-Bass.

Harter, N. (2006). A signpost at the crossroads: Hermeneutics in leadership studies. In S. Huber & M. Harvey (Eds.), *Leadership at the crossroads* (pp. 14–27). College Park, MD: The James MacGregor Burns Academy of Leadership.

Hauser, M. (2006). *Moral minds: How nature designed our universal sense of right and wrong*. New York: HarperCollins.

Heifetz, R. (2006). Anchoring leadership in the work of adaptive progress. In F. Hesselbein & M. Goldsmith (Eds.), *The leader of the future 2* (pp. 73–84). San Francisco: Jossey-Bass.

Hesselbein, F., & Goldsmith, M. (2006). *The leader of the future 2*. San Francisco: Jossey-Bass.

Hesselbein, F., Goldsmith, M., & Beckhard, R. (1996). *The leader of the future: New visions, strategies, and practices for the next era*. San Francisco: Jossey-Bass.

IPCC. (2007). *Climate change 2007: Impacts, adaptation, and vulnerability*. Geneva: WMO & UNEP. [http://www.ipcc.ch/]

IPCC. (2007a). *Contribution of working group 1 to the fourth assessment report of the intergovernmental panel on climate change: Summary for policymakers*. Geneva: WMO & UNEP. [http://www.ipcc.ch/]

James, J. (1996). *Thinking in the future tense*. New York: Simon & Schuster.

Joint Science Academies Statement: Global response to climate change. (2005). Retrieved from http://www.timesonline.co.uk/tol/news/world/article530945.ece

Joireman, J. (2005). Environmental problems as social dilemmas: The temporal dimension. In A. Strathman & J. Joireman (Eds.), *Understanding behavior in the context of time: Theory, research, and application* (pp. 289–304). Mahwah, NJ: Lawrence Erlbaum Associates.

Joireman, J., Strathman, A., & Balliet, D. (2006). Considering future consequences: An integrative model. In J. Sanna & E. Chang (Eds.), *Judgements over time: The interplay of thoughts, feelings, and behaviors* (pp. 82–99). Oxford, UK: Oxford University Press.

Kellerman, B., & Webster, S. (2001). The recent literature on public leadership reviewed and considered. *The Leadership Quarterly, 12*, 485–514.

Kouzes, J., & Posner, B. (2002). *The leadership challenge*. San Francisco: Jossey-Bass.

Machiavelli, N. (1983). *The prince*. New York: Penguin Classics. Originally published in 1513.

Mathias, P. (1969). *The first industrial nation: An economic history of Britain 1700–1914*. New York: Scribner's.

Meadows, D., Meadows, D., Randers, J., & Behrens, W. (1972). *The limits to growth: A report for the Club of Rome's project on the predicament of mankind*. New York: Universe Books.

Meadows, D., Randers, J., & Meadows, D. (2004). *Limits to growth: The 30-year update*. White River Junction, VT: Chelsea Green Publishing Company.

Northouse, P. (2007). *Leadership: Theory and practice*. Thousand Oaks, CA: Sage Publications.

Nowotny, H. (1994). *Time: The modern and postmodern experience.* Cambridge, MA: Polity Press.

Parks, C., & Posey, D. (2005). Temporal factors in social dilemma choice behavior: Integrating interdependence and evolutionary perspectives. In A. Strathman & J. Joireman (Eds.), *Understanding behavior in the context of time: Theory, research, and application* (pp. 225–241). Mahwah, NJ: Lawrence Erlbaum Associates.

Pfeffer, J. (1977). The ambiguity of leadership. *Academy of Management Review, 2*(1), 104–112.

Reading, A. (2004). *Hope and despair: How perceptions of the future shape human behavior.* Baltimore, MD: Johns Hopkins University Press.

Senge, P. (2006). Systems citizenship: The leadership mandate for this millennium. In F. Hesselbein & M. Goldsmith (Eds.), *The leader of the future 2* (pp. 31–46). San Francisco: Jossey-Bass.

Senge, P., Lichtenstein, B., Kaeufer, K., Bradbury, H., & Carroll, J. (2007). Collaborating for systemic change. *MIT Sloan Management Review, 48*(2), 44–53.

Snyder, C., Rand, K., & Ritschel, L. (2006). Hope over time. In J. Sanna & E. Chang (Eds.), *Judgements over time: The interplay of thoughts, feelings, and behaviors* (pp. 100–119). Oxford, UK: Oxford University Press.

Stern, N. (2006). *Stern review: The economics of climate change.* Retrieved from http://www.hmtreasury.gov.uk/independent_reviews/stern_review_economics_climate_change/stern_review_report.cfm

Williams, E. (1961). *Capitalism and slavery.* New York: Russell & Russell.

Winston, B., & Patterson, K. (2006). An integrative definition of leadership. *International Journal of Leadership Studies 1*(2), 6–66.

Zabarenko, D. (2006, March 16). Global warming reaches 'tipping point': Report. *Reuters.* Retrieved from http://www.enn.com/printerfriendly.html?id=10077&cat=today

Zaleski, Z. (2005). Future orientation and anxiety. In A. Strathman & J. Joireman (Eds.), *Understanding behavior in the context of time: Theory, research, and application* (pp. 125–141). Mahwah, NJ: Lawrence Erlbaum Associates.

BENJAMIN W. REDEKOP is Francis Willson Thompson Chair of Leadership Studies and Associate Professor of Social Science in the Department of Liberal Studies at Kettering University (formerly GMI) in Flint, Michigan. He teaches courses in leadership, philosophical ethics, and the history of science, and is a member of the Kettering Industrial Ecology Team, which has been awarded a National Science Foundation grant to develop a multidisciplinary course in industrial ecology. He can be contacted at bredekop@kettering.edu.